Graham Wilson

TOPS OF THE NORTH
Vol II: Carlisle and the Cheviot to the Cat & Fiddle

Drawings by Gerry Dale

Millrace

First published in Great Britain in 2009 by
Millrace
2a Leafield Road, Disley
Cheshire SK12 2JF
www.millracebooks.co.uk

ISBN: 978-1-902173-30-6

Typeset in Adobe Garamond Pro.
Printed and bound in the United Kingdom
by T J International Ltd, Padstow, Cornwall PL28 8RW

Acknowledgements

In Volume I, I acknowledged the assistance I have received from a number of individuals whilst planning and carrying out this walk. Much of their efforts have overlapped into Volume II and thanks are again due. Particularly, once more, to John Goodman for all the help he gave during my route investigations south of Ilkley. I have also received considerable assistance from, and would like to thank, Mike Collister, Dave Golding of CampFour in Macclesfield, Chris Harle, Dudley Hill, Neil Howard, Gerry Moss, Brian Ray and Jim Tait. As ever, my wife, Tricia, has borne most of the burden.

Graham Wilson

Note to Readers

Readers are reminded that although the information in this book is based on the author's own experience, circumstances can change. This is particularly true of hilly countryside, through which the majority of this route passes. It is the individual's responsibility to assess his or her ability to undertake the journey, or any part thereof, in the manner described.

Contents

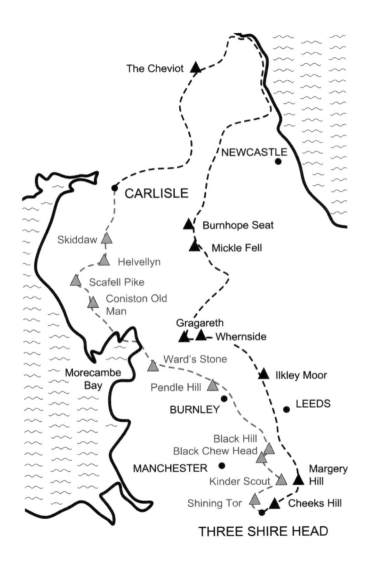

THREE SHIRE HEAD

— 1 —
Wall to wall walking
Carlisle to Twice Brewed

I had arrived at Carlisle in a state of satisfaction.
Seven down, seven to go. All very neat, you might
think. Except it wasn't. If you have just joined us, I had
better explain the story so far. In essence, the concept
of the plan was simple: to create a walk that visited
the highest point of each county in the North of England and to connect these summits with as much high
land—Pendle Hill, Forest of Bowland, Ilkley Moor,
etc—as was practically possible. But there were com-
plications. In 1974 the politicians had decided that
Yorkshire had grown too big for its boots (the County
Cricket Club might not have agreed) and thought
it best if the existing land mass were divided into
three separate counties. Moreover, the noble counties of Cumberland and Westmorland were deemed
too small and destroyed at the stroke of a pen, to be
replaced by Cumbria. As a result, County Tops were
moved around like Chinese Chequers, with some
added and others cast to oblivion. To accommodate
all this gerrymandering, I decided that my itinerary
would have to include all County Tops, both old and

new, that were higher than my starting point of Three Shire Head. (For those about to raise the interrogatory arm of confusion, I can only point them in the direction of the first chapter of Volume I.)

In short, this means there are, in the North of England, fourteen counties either alive or dead and therefore fourteen County Tops. So far I had done seven (four killed off, one reincarnated and two newborn). This left Northumberland (both dead and alive), Durham (dead), Durham (alive), Yorkshire (dead), along with Lancashire, North Yorkshire, South Yorkshire and Staffordshire (all alive and more or less kicking). The more arithmetically agile might calculate this meant there were eight, or possibly nine, Tops left to do and they would be wrong. Northumberland (dead or alive) is the same summit and Mickle Fell has had a more than chequered history. At any given moment it was the highest point in Yorkshire (old) and Durham (new). Depending on Parliamentary procedure, it might have even been the highest point in Cumbria for a few seconds, but we will just let that pass.

Another complication is that although I had reached the farthest north as far as the west was concerned, it was still a long way further north before you reached the highest point of Northumberland

and its adjacent moors, a journey which entails a few miles of cow country to get there and a good few more to get back. There is an odd bump or two, like Fawcet Hill that offers magnificent views but at around 550 feet is more in the molehill than Matterhorn class. Fortunately Northumberland has a number of redeeming features which include Hadrian's Wall and a much becastled coastline. Though not exactly high land as in the original plan, both are well worth a visit, so visit I will, journeying up by the Wall and returning by the county's littoral splendours.

So much for the back-story. Let's on with the motley. There are at least two ways out of Carlisle. One is to follow the line of the Wall through Stanwix, the site of a large Roman cavalry camp, and the village of Tarraby before joining the busy B6264 at the Near Boot Inn (some suitably equestrian reference here, I understand) and thereby crossing the M6. This will appeal to the purist or, as Philip Larkin has it, the 'ruin-bibber, randy for antique'. Alternatively, you can join the official Hadrian's Wall Path that exits via Rickerby Park to the village of that name. This will appeal to those who feel that safety is in signposts. Once started, there is not a great deal to delay the Wallwayers as they are escorted off the premises along a narrow enclosed strip of land that runs close to the road. That is, unless it is a rather forlorn-looking tower that stands in the middle of a field built by one George Head Head. In itself, it offers little interest but you could break the monotony of this

particular passage by pondering over the name of the perpetrator. Among the possibilities you might like to consider is whether its owner was, in fact the 'Head' Head, or Head son of Head, with the sort of superior double-barrelled name that didn't require a hyphen,

or, there again, a moment of creative enthusiasm by the Registrar for Births, Marriages and Deaths. Assuming a sufficiently serious approach to the problem has been taken, you will now have crossed the M6 to reach the village of Linstock. Footpaths alongside the river link up with the Stanegate past the Stag Inn through Crosby-on-Eden, before crossing the A6898 onto the cycleway of Sandy Lane. This in turn joins the antiquarians a little before Wall Head, where a variety of lanes leads directly to Newtown, which appears to signal what the Romans, no doubt, considered the end of civilisation but, to us, that the noteworthy stuff is about to begin.

There is one interesting juxtaposition, however. The track that you are marching along is in fact the course of the Wall, once patrolled by the Legions, and to your immediate south is the rear of that apotheosis of modernity, Carlisle Airport. Probably this feature should more properly be described by the more old-fashioned term 'airfield' (and none the worse for that) as I have seen little aeronautic activity during my various visits. I may be mistaken and perhaps today's Good Burghers of Carlisle jet off to the exotic on a regular basis, but I rather suspect the sheep are not too much troubled by sonic bangs and the like. Anyway, it makes a change from the hidden approaches to most towns, which are characterised by rubbish dumps and scrap-metal yards. Though, given the present economic climate, it may well come to the same thing.

The next few miles are a series of field paths that connect the villages of Walton, with its popular Centurion Inn, Banks and Gilsland. It's at Walton that matters change. Like children's milk teeth, the Wall emerges, at first little more than sunken rocks, then slowly erupting with fresh assertion until at last you and they arrive at Hare Hill where a substantial chunk of Wall appears. On one of the blocks is to be found the carved initials PP. Assuming it was not the work of some Victorian graffitist, these letters meant that the Primus Pilus, the chief centurion of a legion, was signing the work off. While each group of legionaries was responsible for a section of the Wall, the actual manning of the ramparts was not done by Romans wrenched from the vineyards of Tuscany or the sun-drenched beaches of the Adriatic. Once complete (*C'mon lads, the sooner we get this built, the sooner we all get home*), they left it to the Auxiliary Legions, made up from the various tribes that had been conquered to form the Empire. It all sounds all too familiar. A mixture of the EU, UN Police Force and *Aufwiedersehen Pet*.

But the real stuff is at hand. First, a signal station next to a car park that offers sweeping views to the south and west, then a milecastle and remains of two turrets before arriving at the fort of Birdoswald. Thereafter a series of fortlets and turrets stamp their authority on the immediate landscape and then for miles beyond. But this elaborate ha-ha was more than a fortification. It was as much a statement of intent. Hereabouts lies the northerly boundary of the Roman Empire and when it came to boundaries, the Romans, like other animals, liked to leave their identifying mark.

For the Wallites, Birdoswald is up there with the best. It was a full-blown fort which acted as a base for 1,000 soldiers, and recent excavations have unearthed a deal of information. There are the remains of two granaries, a hospital and a unique Basilica which was a sort of sports hall. The Visitor Centre is worth a visit and tells the story of the past 2,000 years, for Birdoswald has, in one form or another, been continually occupied. First, after the Romans had left, as a large timber hall, then a mediaeval tower house. Eventually it became a farm. This was originally fortified against Reivers and Moss Troopers as a bastle house by the Tweddle family, who were probably Reivers themselves, then in more peaceful times gentrified, with its existing mock pele tower erected in 1858. It then remained in the hands of the landed gentry until it was handed over to the, no doubt, grateful nation.

A particular point of interest is its location. The gap between the Wall and the river Irthing is particularly narrow at this point so, built on a rocky spur and with its rear safeguarded by the river valley, it must have been nigh on impregnable. All the more so when the stone wall replacement eventually formed its northern defences. But with every advantage often comes a disadvantage. The river swings north at this point and, for the wall to continue, had to be bridged. The Romans, over time, had three goes at this. Hadrian's first effort lasted only thirty-odd years which, unless an Arturus Scargilius of the day had some of the lads on a work-to-rule, probably says more about the forces of nature than shoddy workmanship. A supposition that is supported by the fact that the original Roman masonry is currently stranded some 200 yards from where the river now runs.

Now that there's something to see, it's probably a good idea to have some grasp as to what the Romans were up to. The Wall was the brainchild of the Emperor Hadrian but, as is so often the case, once the grand design has been announced and the plaudits received, the perpetrator moves on to pastures new, leaving some poor sod, in this case Aulus Platorius Nepos, to sort out the detail. You can picture the Planning Meeting:

Right, chaps, I imagine this will be fairly straightforward. Chuck a bridge across the Tyne somewhere near the sea, then build the wall between it and the Solway Firth. General spec: 15 feet high, 10 feet wide. Usual crenellated fortification, entries for and aft every mille passuum. Intermediate turrets if necessary. Use your discretion here. No point bankrupting the

Empire over this lot. Bit of a shortage of decent building material at the west end so you'll have to make do with turf and timber pro tem. Right, have to go. Any problems, you can catch me in the South of France sorting out the Volcae.

In fact, it was a little more complex than that. As far as the Humber, the Romans had the situation more or less under control, but once they had pushed up North matters changed. A Celtic tribe, the Brigantes, continued to prove rather a handful and any ambition to push into Scotland meant they exposed their rear to attack. During the period of the conquest there were three schools of thought: Agricola, who wanted to render the whole of Britain under Roman rule, Emperor Antonine, who built a wall from Old Kilpatrick on the Firth of Clyde to Falkirk on the Firth of Forth, presumably on the perfectly reasonable assumption that there was little worth fighting for above the Highland Line, and, between them, Hadrian, who realised that pushing up as far as Glasgow meant there was a strong possibility of the Brigantes forming a coalition with the tribes of Southern Scotland and decided the place to draw a line in the sand was between the Solway Firth and the mouth of the river Tyne, where he could keep an eye on both parties.

Once you have been travelling for about seven or eight miles, you will start to suspect that you are walking against the grain. Most pilgrims walk from east to west and the signposts are geared on that assumption. This can be a little disconcerting as what is obvious in one direction is not necessarily so in the opposite. It is quite easy to find your way into habitation, for example, but often less obvious as to how you escape. The bonus is that even at the height of the season your way is more peaceful. In the morning, there are a couple of hours before the advancing vanguard appears in a flurry of thick tweed stockings and bobbling headwear and you switch on your pre-set *Morning! Lovely/Dreadful weather! Have a good day!* machine. Then, in the evening, as the late-starters or those overburdened with the type of equipment suitable for a trek across the Kalahari eventually plod mournfully by, stillness descends. You again have the place to yourself, and the wildlife once more comes out of hiding. Also, if the *Dreadful!* element has been in full swing, you have had the advantage of the weather at your back.

When I last walked this stretch one late April, I experienced some interesting weather. I left Walton in a drizzle of sleet. By the time I reached Birdoswald, I was down to shirt-sleeves and veered slightly off route into Gilsland, hoping to find some shade and refreshment. Disappointed, I toiled up the hill under the railway that runs from Carlisle to Newcastle and back onto the route. Matters changed again. First a jumper was replaced, then a fleece, then, as hail started to fall, full waterproofs. This was proper hail, real ball-bearing stuff. Temperature rising by a critical degree or two, dry hail turns to torrential rain. Where the Wall Path is joined by the Pennine Way and unzipped cagoule pockets started to fill with water, I called it a day and slutched my way to the Greenhead Hotel.

Derobed, with hands wrapped around a mug of soup, I found a seat by the window. Within seconds the late afternoon sunlight was streaming in. Well, as they say in these parts, if you're not happy with the weather, just hang around for half an hour. Later that evening I had to visit Brampton. As I approached Low Row, where the road notoriously dips and twists, I noticed a strip of pasture that appeared to have been heavily limed. On arrival I found that the 'lime' was in fact over three inches of snow and the cause of a scene of mayhem. Cars collided, artics jack-knifed, motorbikes thrown casually into ditches. Half a mile later, back to lambs on warm green grass. The odd thing about the whole affair was that the strip of snow was completely regular, as if some giant hand had been marking out a football pitch.

Just before Greenhead, the Pennine Way joins the Wall and we shall stay with it until we reach the top of Cheviot. It had been my original hope to avoid this much trodden pathway but even a careful examination of the relevant maps did not offer much in the way of alternative. As I will explain later, being caught in the open was not a good idea around these parts, so the number of rights of way established through trade and other necessities were extremely limited. It is possible to leave the wall around Greenhead and work your way north on rights of way to the junction of Scotland and England at Carter Bar, but there were a number of reasons why I decided against it. First, from the walking point of view, you would miss the best part of the Wall. Second, at Carter Bar, such is the proximity of the Border, you would have little choice other than joining the Pennine Way for its final thirty-mile assault on Cheviot. Third, the paths, such as they may be, pass through Kielder Forest.

I am not against walking through woods. In fact they can offer a very welcome respite from the elements— but 'Forest' in England tends to mean conifers and usually a fair number of them. This is particularly true if, as in this case, the Forest covers 250 square miles. It also churns out half a million cubic metres of timber a year, which by anybody's reckoning is an awful lot of chipboard. The Government started planting in the 1920s as a method of re-employing men laid off from the shipping and mining industries. Like Topsy, it just grew, covering the moors that had once been home to sheep and grouse. There is high land here. Peel Fell rises to nearly 2,000 feet and Sighty Crag has the dubious distinction of being the English Marilyn that is farthest from a road. Both appear on the map to be marooned in a sea of pine. There are tracks marked on the map but I am suspicious of them. In a working forest matters change quickly and the OS can equally quickly become out of date. If things go wrong, you can soon find yourself floundering in the undergrowth and on very wet ground. Once started, you are committed. There is no way you can get an overview of the terrain and, even over short distances, the whole experience can be very frustrating. At around thirty miles it could try the patience of the most imperturbable Sisyphus.

And there is another difficulty. Slap in the middle is Kielder Water, with its twenty-seven miles of shoreline. So your route must be carefully planned to avoid getting your feet wet. It was originally built to augment the water supplies of the river Tees and meet the demands of ICI and the steel works. But industrial practice has changed and it has only had to reinforce the Tees on two occasions. What appears to have been built is the biggest boating lake in the world. Those in charge seem to be doing their best with a bad job but you can't help feeling that the whole affair is little more than a white elephant.

To be fair, the area does act as a sanctuary for more acceptable types of fauna and Kielder Forest is one of the last strongholds for the red squirrel. But even the chance of my playing a bit-part in a Beatrix Potter movie offered scarce compensation for the probable alternatives. And certainly not if it meant that some of the best walking in Northumberland was to be ignored. There are still antiquities to be noted hereabouts (and even found—a postman as late as 1915 picked up what he thought was an old bucket that turned out to be a bronze Roman dry measure in perfect condition) but even the most ardent Wallite will raise his eyes during this passage. All ridge walks are good but the best are those that climb and fall suddenly, releasing the view of what is to come, then just as suddenly switching it off. From Thirlwall Nicks to Cuddy's Crags, such is the walk beside the Wall. From Greenhead it slowly ascends until it reaches Windshields Crags, the highest point on the Wall.

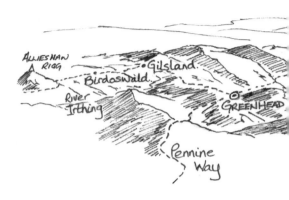

Here you can look north towards Cheviot and the surrounding Otterburn and Rothbury Moors, and there is a sense that you are in the high lands again. Sadly, this will only continue for ten miles and then, regardless of the actual altitude, you feel that once more you are in lowland farm country. But while it is there, it is good.

Perhaps one of the best places to stand and stare is from the car park at Steel Rigg. The OS marks this with a Viewpoint symbol and such an accolade it richly deserves. Now you can observe what no traveller can see from the B6318. From there, the Wall appears to undulate gracefully across the horizon, supported by gently rising pastures. But from where

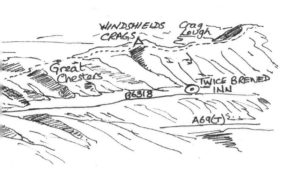

we stand, there is an entirely different view. Some Ice Age has gouged the softer rock, leaving the harder dolerite of the Whin Sill as a perpendicular edge. It rarely rises above 100 feet but the columnar structure and the uniform steepness give a flattering sense of precipice.

It is rock designed for climbing and—not surprisingly—High Shield Crag was the cradle of Northumbrian rock climbing. The first ascents of the more obvious lines were recorded in the 1912 Climbers' Club Journal and no less a figure than Geoffrey Winthrop Young commented in his introduction to the original guidebook that 'There is no nobler country ... as it rolls ... in great waves of historic moorland, cresting upon the skyline into sudden and surprising crags.' It's where I first started climbing and although the rock structure lent itself to the grip'n'pull technique (nomenclature like 'Tarzan' gives the game away) this was of little use when it came to the subtleties of gritstone. Nevertheless, I always felt the longer climbs were more than just problems. You seemed to work your way around the rock architecture as you did on the much larger cliffs of the Lake District or North Wales. It now appears little used and somewhat dilapidated, but none the less dear for all that.

The cliff is commonly known as Crag Lough, after the lochan that lies at its foot. This, along with the Loughs of Broomlee and Greenlee, is a further gem invisible to those rushing from Newcastle to Carlisle and, as you stand on top of any of the crags looking down on a land moated by splashes of swan-strewn water, you get the feeling that Hadrian had got it about right. Where you are standing is definitely the edge of something and northwards is probably somewhere else.

If you get the impression I am giving this section especial prominence, you would not be wrong. A few years ago, in an interview at the Kendal Mountaineering Festival, I made a rather throwaway comment to the effect that there was no rock climbing in the North East of England. What I had meant was that for somebody who lived, as I did, in Sunderland, there were no easily accessible rock faces, which is the reason why I travelled to the Lakes. What followed was reminiscent of a scene from *The Hustler*. After my turn was done, I repaired to the Gents, where I was approached by several wide-shouldered men with even broader Northumbrian accents who had taken exception to my slight on their county. I tried to explain, but it was made transparently clear that if I didn't know what I was takking aboot, I shood had me gob.

Being no Paul Newman and anxious to make amends, I went about procuring a copy of *No Nobler County* (the readjustment from GWY was deliberate): *A celebration of climbing in Northumberland*, published by the Northumbrian MC. As well as telling me about the range of climbing in the county, it explained the genesis and history of the Club. It is well worth acquiring if you can lay your hands on it, for it also contains a selection of articles that originally appeared in the Club's newsletter. There is a level of forthrightness that you'd expect from people in these parts, which encourages a lively prose style. I particularly liked the verve of 'Geordies—"Keepers of the County"' by Bob Smith and the wry reminiscence of a climbing widow who, on her husband's return some time after midnight, was somewhat put off by the cosmetic whiff of his latest *Eau d'Escalade*.

One thing has not changed from the days of my earlier excursions. This area is still remote and you have to plan your arrangements with some care. So this might be an appropriate moment to pause and take stock. If you follow the road from Steel Rigg to the B6318 you will arrive at Twice Brewed. Here you will find a multiplicity of overnight stays, campsite, Youth Hostel, B&B and the hotel itself. It is not impossible you will visit the last named, regardless of where your bed is, and you might wonder about the name. The popular explanation is that when General Wade's men were building the Military Road they found the beer too weak and demanded that it be brewed for a second time to increase the strength. Apparently this is brewing nonsense and the more likely explanation is that it is a corruption of Twa Brews, the twin hills a traveller would see on his approach.

— 2 —

Saints and sinners
Twice Brewed to Bamburgh

There is one great advantage in breaking your journey at Twice Brewed. The next day gets the perfect kick-start. You retread the minor road to the foot of Peel Crags, where an interesting little scramble known as the Cat Steps returns you to the switchback. The Wall from Highshield Crags to Hotbank Crags is rather un-Romanlike. Instead of the unforgiving straight line, the fortification moulds itself to the Whin Sill, which at this moment is curving gently to the north. The retrospect from Hotbank is extremely fine and, not surprisingly, much photographed. It forms a fine complement to the shot from Steel Rigg. It is a view for all seasons but is probably at its best on a bright winter's day when the cracks and ledges with which the crag abound are fretted with snow and the light catches the fingering ice as it grips the reeds in the lough beneath.

Although we now go north, the Wallites will be straining at the leash to continue east. For within less than a mile lies Housesteads or, to give it its Sunday name, Vercovicium. This is the finest and best preserved of all the forts along the Wall. In its day it was a busy place and not much has changed. Indeed, at times, it seems to be no more than a child repository for an educational system that has run out of steam.

'Year 9 is getting a little out of hand, Headmaster.'

'Better organise a trip. Bloody Governors' Meeting tomorrow.'

'The Wall as usual, Headmaster?'

Having been through the 'Housesteads Experience' myself, it merely confirms my opinion that the more you force-feed children with culture the more likely they are to reject it. As with most aspects of education, the trick is to let them think they discovered it for themselves.

For those demanding further details, there is already information aplenty but it would be a serious omission if I were to move on without mentioning the name of John Clayton. A Victorian lawyer, later Town Clerk of Newcastle, he first took an interest in the Wall when staying at his family country house, Chesters. He quickly realised that what remained of Hadrian's efforts was in great danger of disappearing altogether, as the locals, regarding it as a monumental cornucopia, plundered the carefully cut stones for a variety of purposes. Thirlwall Castle, for example,

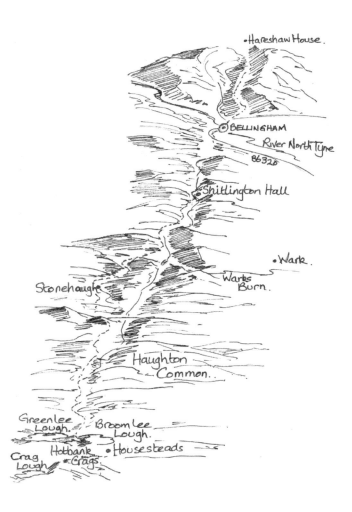

Hareshaw House.

BELLINGHAM

River North Tyne

B6320

Shitlington Hall

Wark.

Warks
Burn.

Stonehaugh

Haughton
Common.

Greenlee
Lough.

Broomlee
Lough.

Crag
Lough.

Hotbank
Crags.

Housesteads

which we passed after leaving Greenhead, owes its existence to the ready-made material that lay to hand, and Wade's engineers in need of hardcore for their road had put Roman endeavours to good use, often building on the selfsame line. Clayton was enough of a lawyer to realise that he couldn't prevent landowners doing as they wished with their own property and decided that the only option was to buy the land and re-site the existing farmhouses out of harm's way.

The outcome was that he saved the distinctive central section. A walk along the top of the Whin Sill would be invigorating in its own right and the discovery and examination of ancient remains would be similarly interesting. But it is the combination of the two that gives the walk its unique circumstance and makes Hadrian's Wall what it is.

Clayton also excavated the Fort at Chesters, during which evidence was unearthed to resolve a long-standing academic argument. The dig revealed that the Twentieth Legion had been among the workforce when the Wall was built, thus dating the construction to the time of Hadrian and not, as had been more commonly supposed, during the occupation of Severus nearly a century later. The latter, in fact, had done little more than a general refurb job. I don't know if John Clayton was a drinking man but, if he was, he probably cracked open a decent bottle or two at the time.

We now return to Rapishaw Gap and quickly realise that the winter that enhanced the photograph could have a further advantage. The ground hereabouts is generally marshy and conditions underfoot are much improved when the ground temperature has fallen below zero. Afforestation has yet to stretch its tentacles over the majority of the next stage to Bellingham but there is enough of it to let you decide for yourself whether a major trek through the trees of Kielder would have been preferable to your march along the Wall. Not that the way before you is anything other than pretty desolate, and little must have changed over the centuries. You may have gathered from the opening chapter that the land north of the Wall had not been the most peaceful of places. Two warring neighbours used it as their killing fields—the empty spaces of Otterburn and Flodden stand as witness—and the Northern Marches became a buffer zone between the two nations. But Nature abhors a vacuum and soon the gap was filled by the 'great riding families', the members of which gloried in such names as Nebless Clem, Ill Drooned Geordie and Buggerback. Although their descendants are now established local families held in high esteem, at the time they were little more than thieves and cattle rustlers or, as contemporary legal records had it, 'a perverse and crooked people' given to 'outragious forradging'.

No one was safe from these Reivers or Moss Troopers. In order to establish some sort of control, successive governments tried dividing the area into Marches, each regulated by its own March Warden. This looked pretty good on paper but as the plan usually involved moving up impartial southerners to take charge, it caused a certain amount of local resentment. If, on the other hand, northerners were appointed, they more often than not, as in the case of the notorious Sir John Foster, used their special knowledge to turn the office to personal gain. To further complicate matters there was, in addition to the violence fuelled by neighbouring feuds, a larger political overview. Scotland had traditionally allied itself with England's enemies and, before they could 'busy giddy minds with foreign quarrels', English monarchs had to make certain they had not left the back door off the sneck. Henry VIII, for example, deliberately encouraged trouble in the region to keep the Scots occupied, demanding the Moss Troopers, 'his picked and chosen men', should 'make a raid at least once a week while grass is on the ground'.

Clearly it was a case of every man for himself and those who could not count on the collective security of the towns had to look to an architect who understood the score. What you had built depended on your circumstance. The better off had tower houses or peles, the less well off but still relatively prosperous relied on bastles. Both were designed on the same principle. A heavily-fortified ground floor that could secure the livestock, and upper floors that provided living accommodation for the family. Walls were up to four feet thick and in the case of the pele towers there was an outer defensive stone wall or 'barmkin', with the stairs to the upper floors of the tower itself spiralling upwards in a clockwise direction to allow a right-handed defender the advantage when it came to sword play. In addition, there was usually a 'trip step' that was much steeper than the others and in the poor light could cause many a misjudgement by the uninitiated. The downmarket version was the bastle, a massively built farmhouse with the ground floor for livestock (an early form of underfloor heating) and access to the living quarters by a ladder that could be easily withdrawn. Despite all these precautions, attacks could prevail. The most common method was through 'scumfishing', the use of sodden straw to smoke out the inhabitants.

After you have crossed Warks Burn, the route becomes more obvious, often following well-used tracks and lanes. In fact, the final mile of this section is along a main road. Eventually you reach Bellingham. Like so many habitations in these parts, the buildings tend to keep their heads down. None more so than St Cuthbert's Church. A squat building, it unusually has a roof made of massive stone slabs supported by stone arches which, in turn, have to be sustained by heavy buttressing. Its construction reflects its geography. The chancels of thirteenth-century churches normally had timber roofs, which the invading Scots took delight in setting on fire. Eventually the locals tired of replacing the woodwork and built what, in effect, was an artificial cave.

In the churchyard there is a curious gravestone shaped in the form of a pedlar's pack. It is reputed to be a tomb that indicates that trouble could as easily come from within as without. 'The Tale of the Long Pack' is part of local folklore and was the source of a short story written by the Ettrick Shepherd, James Hogg. The essence of the story is that a Colonel Ridley, having made his fortune in India, retired to Lee Hall in 1723. One bitter winter's evening, while he and his family were in London, leaving the hall manned by only a skeleton staff, a pedlar appeared begging for a bed. The housekeeper refused him entry but, given his state of exhaustion, allowed him to leave his pack until the morning, while he searched for lodging elsewhere.

Eventually curiosity got the better of the servant and she started to examine the pack which, to her horror, began to move. Her screams of anxiety were answered by a farmhand who fired at the pack with a gun he had been using to scare off the local hoodies. Blood oozed from the canvas and they discovered that the long pack contained a now-dead man. This wooden horse had clearly been planted to allow others to gain access to the property and the about-to-be-invaded set about gathering others to help defend Lee Hall and the not inconsiderable wealth that lay within. Eventually, at what must have been a prearranged time, horses were heard. As they entered the courtyard, the attackers were duly ambushed and in the carnage many must have been killed. However, when daylight broke, not a body was to be found; nor, more to the point, were several members of so-called respectable families in the district ever seen again.

The fifteen miles of Pennine Way from Bellingham to Byrness offers the same terrain as before, except that in Redesdale Forest you have the added excitement of being run over by forestry vehicles who appear to see themselves as a heavyweight equivalent to the mountain bikers that frequent the much-vaunted Kielder trails further west. The final mile gives a pleasant walk along the river Rede, a much-needed change from what one guidebook describes as a possible film scenario for a post-nuclear landscape.

But if, on your way to Byrness, you require something to distract your mind, you can consider the following day. Before you leave this last point of habitation it is best, once more, to have a pretty precise game plan. The next stop is Wooler and, as we have to go by the summit of Cheviot, Wooler is getting on for thirty miles away. The Fit and Furious will of course just bash on. The more circumspect might consider the alternatives. The most romantic solution is to leave the pub after a good meal and get a few miles under your belt by walking uphill until it gets dark. Curl up in the heather until you can strike out with the dawn chorus in your ears and the breeze in your hair. This, after the third pint, is what is known as 'a good idea' and you might even get away with it. But the probability is that you will be sharing your bed with a temporarily-dammed stream and the dawn's gentle zephyr is gusting at around Force 8. Names like Windy Gyle were not born of affection. It is best

RAVENS KNOWE

BYRNESS

River
Rede

A68(T)

Redesdale
Forest

PADON HILL

LORD'S SHAW

Hareshaw House

to remember that bivouacking is an art and should not be undertaken lightly.

A second solution is to break your journey at Uswayford. An old drove road, Clennell Street, cuts across the Pennine Way one mile north-east of Russell's Cairn and leads eastwards for a mile and a half to the only possible B&B en route (and it goes without saying you would have to book in advance). If you were to stay here, you would break your journey to Wooler into two more manageable stages. If you have had enough of the Pennine Way, there would be no need to retrace your steps as the right of way leads east until you are clear of the trees, whereafter you can plot your own route to the head of Harthope Burn and then reach Cheviot via Cairn Hill. It should be mentioned there are also two rudimentary shelters in the vicinity, the first about three or four hours out of Byrness and the second on the way down to Kirk Yetholm. They are only of use in an emergency but may be of comfort if you find yourself more furious than fit.

At some point in all this you will stand on the top of Muckle Cheviot, which at 2,674 feet is the highest point in England outside Cumbria. Despite all our efforts, we are still standing west of the original starting point of Three Shire Head though, as some compensation, it is alleged this particular viewpoint is the only place in England where you can discern both the Irish Channel and the North Sea. It is, as the albatross flies, a mere sixty-odd miles which, if it were a Wandering Albatross at top speed, would take little more than the same number of minutes. Not, mind you, that I've seen much in the way of albatross on Cheviot. To round off this Compendium of Little Known but Nevertheless Useful Facts, there was a time when, along with the Munroist's nemesis on the Cuillin Ridge and Black Hill in the Peak, this particular County Top could earn the epithet of inaccessible. I struggled towards the summit one wet walking holiday only to be denied the final glory by what appeared to be thigh-deep glutinous peat. It might have been deeper. I gave up when the ooze started to approach the knees. The said F&F would, of course, have stood no such infirmity of purpose but leopard-crawled across in triumph. Today there is little problem in reaching the summit cairn. Paved walkways avoid the bog.

Talking of leopard crawls brings back powerful and somewhat painful memories. The crawl is a military manoeuvre whereby you gain ground without the enemy spotting you. It consists of lying prone and maintaining forward motion through the energetic

use of the elbows. As part of my educational process, I had to join the school's CCF and every year these stalwarts repaired to the Otterburn Moors to take part in what was inappropriately termed a Field Day. Fields mean grass, with or without cows. Fields do not mean intransigent heather firmly rooted in peat bog. The general tactic seemed to be that each platoon of would-be leopards crawled from one indeterminate point to another, then waited for an equally indeterminate message from the Signal Section, before repeating the process *ad nauseam*. I am sure that leopards can make very satisfactory progress on what ever passes for their elbows, but my observation of wildlife programmes makes me equally certain that they are not required to carry firearms. I was. By this I do not mean one of those ultra-light James Bond type of firearm but a 303 rifle of the sort used during the Battle of the Somme, which had now filtered down the military food chain to the school cadet corps. Size, like time, is relative. I was small and the rifle was big and, but for my waterlogged battledress, would have been a good deal heavier than its bearer. My initial reaction was to throw the wretched thing in the nearest ditch but childhood reading had convinced me that to abandon arms in the British Army meant instant death, so there was no choice but to struggle on. Eventually I was allowed to give up being a leopard and adopt a posture that more resembled an early stage of Emerson's rise of man and, at some distance behind my confrères, stumbled back to base dragging my rifle behind me. Bump. Bump. Bump. Very A A Milne.

I retell this story, not to elicit sympathy or even scorn, but as a general warning about the nature of the Northumbrian Moors. At the top of Cheviot you will, for the first time since Carlisle, have abandoned the security blanket of carefully sited signposts. As a result, you are on your own until you reach Wooler, and if you wander off piste you can very easily find yourself the other way round, as it were. It is rough ground covered with tenacious heather—blooming is a totally inadequate expletive to describe it—and sprinkled with ankle-breaking rockeries delicately disguised by ferns. Actually, if you keep your head, matters are not over-bad. There is a well-worn track to Scald Hill, after which it is not too difficult to join landrover tracks and the like that lead past the building at Broadstruther to cross the burn of that name. A pleasant climb through a wood (red squirrels here) and rights of way lead to Wooler Common, and then via Kenterdale Hill into the streets of your eventual destination.

Somewhere around Wooler Common you may have noticed the reappearance of waymark signs.

These bear a Celtic cross and signify that you have joined St Cuthbert's Way, which connects the Southern Upland Way to Lindisfarne on the east coast of Northumberland. Cuthbert was a much-travelled man and made this journey to persuade the Celtic Christians of the North that they should accept the ruling of the Synod of Whitby and follow the practices of Roman Rite. Once this had been completed, he retired to hermithood and, after rejecting a couple of apparently unnecessarily comfortable des res, settled on Farne Island. We will remain under this saint's protection until we reach the cave which bears his name, whereat he passes the baton to St Oswald who will lead us through the rest of our journey until, once more, we are safely behind Hadrian's Wall.

Death did not mean the end of Cuthbert's peregrinations. He was buried in Lindisfarne Priory but in 875 the monks, alarmed by the Danish invasion, gathered together their valuables, which included the body of St Cuthbert, and for seven years wandered around Northumbria seeking a safe haven. Eventually a church was built at Chester-le-Street. A century later the Danes reappeared and the process was repeated until the party reached the monastery at Ripon where Cuthbert had been Master 300 years before. Then, once peace had been established, they set off to return to Chester-le-Street, but when Durham was reached the oxen-drawn cortège refused to budge and, taking this as a sign that Cuthbert felt enough was enough, a church (later the cathedral)

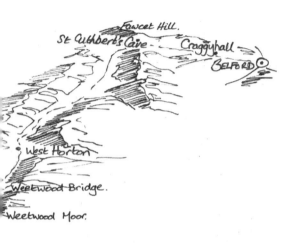

was built to house the mortal remains. There, apart from a quick trip to Lindisfarne to avoid the Harrying of the North and a game of hide-and-seek during the Reformation, they stayed and are there, allegedly incorrupt, to this very day. From any standpoint, it makes our journey from Byrness to Wooler appear a mere bagatelle.

Wooler, as with most places around here, is not architecturally very prepossessing. Despite its known existence from 1107, there is nothing in the way of medieval grace or Jacobean elegance to catch the eye. Being so far north, this was in the firing line and raiding parties from both sides of the Border regarded it as fair game, burning it down on a regular basis.

We leave Wooler via the bowling club and Glendale Middle School to face an initially steep, then brackeny rise onto Weetwood Moor. Unlike most moorland, this is surprisingly cultivated, consisting of plantations, fenced fields and the obligatory cows. Once up, you then go down the other side, thrashing your way through still more bracken. I expect St C, unless he was in a particularly self-flagellatory mood, took the rather easier option at valley level. Follow the footsteps of the English army on its way to Flodden Field and cross the river Till over the interesting Weetwood Bridge, whence a minor road allows you to reach the settlements of West and East Horton.

Once the Way has crossed Hetton Burn to reach the rather indeterminate area known as Hazelrigg, there is an alternative. The quicker route to Belford is to leave St C as soon as is feasible and travel in a more or less straight line along a path and bridleway to Swinhoe Farm. I would, however, continue in the saint's steps until they reach Fawcet Hill, and then turn to make your way to Swinhoe. The blessings are threefold. First it gives you a chance to examine St Cuthbert's Cave. If he did in fact choose this spot for his meditations, then he knew what he was doing. On the west side of a wooded slope, it is sheltered from the bitter east wind and through the clearing in the trees he would have had splendid views of Cheviot and its adjacent satellites as they fall away to the Border. Second, the seaward views from Fawcet Hill are worth a visit in their own right. Given a fine day, they offer a tremendous introduction to the coast and castles to come.

Once saintly batons have been exchanged, a track leads under the gorse bank into and through a bluebell wood to the third and perhaps finest of the benisons on offer. Swinhoe Lake is only a snapshot from the track but, framed by drooping branches, the water-fowl scuttle around imperious swans as the harsh croak of pheasants echoes around the wooded banks. Continue past the lake to Swinhoe Farm, then over fields to lanes leading into Belford. A good place to pause and admire the attractions of its square, with its eighteenth-century coaching inn, the Blue Bell, for so long a stopping point on the Great North Road.

As we shall discover, despite the macho-culture of the area, daughters played a significant part in the history of this corner of the North East. Grace

Darling is the most renowned but she was not the only girl of spirit in these parts. Another was Grissell, daughter of Sir John Cochrane. Dad had made the mistake of joining the wrong side in Monmouth's rebellion, with the outcome that he was now awaiting execution in Edinburgh. Little could prevent it other than an intercession by a third party who had the King's ear, plus, of course, a large sum of money. But the proverbial sands were running out. The death warrant must by now be drawn and on its way up the said Great North Road. All was lost. Grissell thought otherwise. Time clearly was of the essence, so she deduced that the simplest expedient was to delay the arrival of the warrant. She did this by disguising herself as a highwayman and robbing any passing Royal Mail of its contents. Her stand and delivery allowed a sufficient hiatus for £5,000 to change hands and a royal pardon to arrive. Hurrah!

The following section from Belford to Bamburgh turned out to be much more interesting than I had envisaged. I suppose the inverse of the idea that expectation beggars belief. Unlike some stretches of farm country, it throws up something just when you think you're going to get bored. The opening salvo, however, as you are shepherded through the golf course alongside Belford Burn, does not offer much hope. What interest there is seems to be centred around the industrial site of a co-operative granary, followed by dicing with death. The first is not as desperate as you might imagine—they've even planted a few bluebells—but crossing the A1, then the main line from King's Cross to Edinburgh, requires a little more thought. The motor car travelling at 60mph on a single carriageway might, with care, be dodgeable; an express train travelling more than twice as fast on any one of a multiplicity of lines is not. But help is at hand. Railtrack, recognising the sanctity of St Oswald, has installed a telephone and all you have to do is to ring some chap who gives the required information. Comfortingly, this seems to work at a human level rather than the *Your call may be recorded for training purposes. Please choose one of the following options. To cross safely, PRESS ONE. To live dangerously, PRESS TWO* variety.

Field tracks and bits of road lead to Spindlestone Ducket. This lighthouse-shaped building is a bit of an enigma. The OS has it marked as a windmill, whereas 'ducket', like 'doocat' in Scotland, is the local word for dovecote. If it were the latter, it must be the Ritz of dovecotes, for now, according to the brochure, it is elegant, self-catering accommodation comprising kitchen, lounge, bedroom and observatory-cum-

43

library, one on each floor. The views from the top will rival those from Fawcet Hill, but come a tad more expensive.

Follow the road down to Waren Burn before turning left to climb through the woods to Spindlestone Heughs. Here be dragons. Or here was a dragon. Or, to be more precise, the Laidley Worm. Worms in those days weren't useful little creatures that aerated the soil but loathsome scaly serpentine monsters. In fact, the loathsome scaly etc was a rather attractive young lady called Margaret and she found herself in her changed state when she got mixed up in a northern version of the Snow White saga. Usual plot. King marries beautiful second wife who turns out to be a bit miffed when she discovers that in a score out of ten the local lads prefer King's even more beautiful daughter. Second wife, aka Wicked Stepmother, through one method or another puts competition out of the running. In this case, with a bit of thrice-repeated loathsome worm metastasis. Eventually the proper order is returned by some passing thrice-kissing Handsome Prince and WS is turned into a thrice-loathsome toad.

Dragons in the form of Worms have made this part of England their own, the most famous account being the Lambton version and the rather cavalier approach shown by Young Lambton when it came to the preservation of wildlife. Actually 'The Various Chronicles of a Variety of Worms' can cover quite a lot of corners. As with the Pendle Witches, worms can be blamed for personal inadequacy: *Not my fault, guv. It was the Worm wot done it.* Their existence proves that the impoverished really have to rely on the upper classes to solve the particularly tricky problems in life (cf Handsome Prince) and so have a duty to do as they are told. Moreover, the moral of the tale contains a suitable caveat on second marriages. Finally, as Mr Disney discovered to our cost, it is a good story with which to quell fractious children who have been dragged out on a family picnic.

Ignore the signs at the entrance to the caravan site that try to steer you from your legal rights into a field of over-inquisitive bullocks and soon Bamburgh Castle hoves into sight. It can be reached by a circuitous route around the golf course, with even more views across Budle Bay to Lindisfarne and the Farne Islands. For those who wish neither to annoy the golfers—who can be quite as fractious as cows or small children—nor delay a visit to the local hostelry, there is a direct route along the verge of the often busy B1342.

— 3 —

Oh, I do like to be beside the seaside
Bamburgh to Hexham

As they have been on the radar for the last few miles, it is probably a good thing to have a word or two about the Farne Islands. This group comprises twenty-eight islets composed of the same stuff as the cliff at Crag Lough and with a similar columnar structure. As a result, they break the surrounding sea into guts or churns through which, at certain heights of the tide, the water rushes with great power. This maelstrom, coupled with the disappearance of most of the rocks at high water, turned this scattering of dolerite into a haven for wildlife and contemplative monks—and anything but for passing seafarers.

The most notorious of numerous wrecks was the steamship Forfarshire, and the consequent rescue of eight men and a woman by William Darling, keeper of the Longstone Lighthouse, and his daughter, Grace. On 5th September 1838, the vessel had left Hull for Dundee. The boiler failed and the captain, now relying entirely on sail, sought shelter between the Farne Islands and the mainland. Unfortunately, he had mistaken the Longstone for that on the Inner

Farne and, instead of finding relative sanctuary, crashed into the rocky cliffs of Big Harcar.

Judging by the theatrical output of the day, the Victorians liked melodrama, a good dollop of Blood and Thunder interspersed with violent appeals to the emotions. Yet even better than the boards of Drury Lane was the real thing. Grace became a national heroine and a fund was set up to reward her which generated more than £700. Medals were struck and poems penned. Even Wordsworth ('A guardian spirit, sent from pitying heaven / In woman's shape') got in on the act. The story quickly evolved that it was she who, having spotted the wreck from her bedroom window, had persuaded her father to launch the rescue and it was her bravery and fortitude alone that saved the day. Inevitably Art and Life became inextricably confused and *Wreck at Sea*, no doubt complete with nine poor marooned souls, one with her two dead children in her arms, was staged at the Adelphi Theatre. Grace herself was offered a part, with a reported fee of anything between £10 and £80 per performance. The fact that she declined probably gives a truer insight into her character than any version conjured amongst the flickering footlights.

The actuality seems to have been less theatrical and certainly less clear cut. Grace's sister, Thomasin, whilst agreeing that Grace might well have been eager to help, wrote that her father would not have attempted the impracticable and that he certainly wasn't 'the man to endanger her life and his own in weak concession to girlish importunity'. The North Sunderland lifeboat, which included amongst its crew one of Grace's brothers, had also attended the wreck, making an even more hazardous journey. It was unable to return to port, and put up at the Lighthouse until the storm eased. There is a suggestion there was a bitter row between William Darling and the North Sunderland crew over the matter of salvage and that the latter was denied refuge within the lighthouse itself. As to whether the disaster was the result of misfortune or misjudgement is also open to question. At the first inquest it was decided that the captain was culpably negligent as he knew about the faulty boiler and had allowed greed to override prudence. Yet by the time the final body was washed up, the dust had settled and, with greater consideration given to the circumstances, the captain was exonerated.

Overlooking this scene of triumph and disaster was Bamburgh Castle. In fact, it was a lookout on the east turret of the castle who alerted the lifeboatmen at North Sunderland. Nor would it have been the first time maritime disaster had been spotted from these

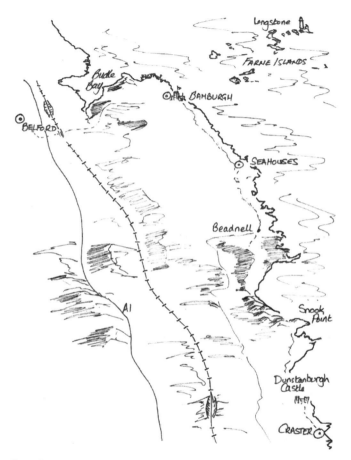

fortified heights. As the capital of the kingdom of Bryneich or Bernicia, the site had been occupied from the sixth century and, over the years, ownership had ping-ponged between the Brits, Saxons and Danes. As usual, the Normans got a grip and, apart from a couple of locals, it stayed in the hands of the Royal Family until it was finally destroyed by artillery during the Wars of the Roses. It remained a partial ruin until it was bought by William Armstrong (of whom more later) and restored to its present rather Disneyfied state. In addition to Bamburgh, we shall also visit the castles at Dunstanburgh and Warkworth, neither of which has suffered so much by way of a makeover.

To connect this fortified chain, there follows nearly thirty miles of coastal footpath, but from time to time it is possible to abandon the official route and walk along the seashore. The first section, from Bamburgh to Seahouses, offers this option. The latter is somewhat of an anomaly in these parts. Whilst most of the former fishing villages retired into nostalgia, Seahouses threw off such a humble mantle and had, and possibly still has, ambitions to be a seaside resort. It has the usual accoutrements, fish and chips, penny arcades and fractious children squabbling over half-sucked sticks of rock and, in the opinion of the author, is perhaps best passed through. If, however, you do intend to loiter, the Olde Ship, with its old-fashioned bars doubling as museums of nautical memorabilia, is well worth a visit. If you don't, thread your way diligently around the inevitable golf course and caravan site to Beadnell.

Beadnell is the social antithesis of Seahouses, and the walk from here to Craster is arguably the best section of the coastline walk. It starts modestly enough through a caravan park but soon stretches out alongside Newton Links, a Site of Special Scientific Interest that protects one of the best examples of vegetated sand dunes. A saltmarsh sanctuary, home to the little tern, lies to the west of Long Nanny Burn. Other curious names intermingle with the flora and fauna. Lobster Carr might be self-evident, but Snook Point, Football Hole and Faggot defy obvious etymological explanation. Then, almost without warning, the path swoops down to Low Newton-by-the-Sea.

This delightful village, now owned by the National Trust, consists of a traditional green surrounded on three sides by fishermen's cottages. The fourth side is a sandy beach. In the top right-hand corner lies what used to be known as the Smack Inn. Doubtless this nomenclature caused confusion to the preponderance of landlubbers who ramble along this stretch of the seaboard and it was changed to the more prosaic 'Ship'. But in no other way is it commonplace. It has its own micro-brewery with a variety of beers on offer. Its fully deserved reputation for food means the appropriately simple furnishings are always occupied and pre-booking is essential for an evening meal. At the right time of the year, local lobsters are known to climb out of the sea right onto your plate.

The walk from Newton to Craster is dominated by the bare, ruined fangs of Dunstanburgh Castle. Built by the second Duke of Lancaster at the beginning of the fourteenth century, this northern Camelot was conceived half as safe retreat, half Arthurian-inspired 'joyous garde'. It failed on both counts. Lancaster was captured and beheaded for his part in a rebellion against the king and the castle quickly fell into disrepair. Attempts were made at restoration but continual attacks during the Wars of the Roses eventually did for it. A romantic enterprise covering eleven acres and perched on a rocky fastness, it has spent well over twice as long as a ruin as it did fulfilling its twin function of bastion and dream.

The village of Craster appears yet another archetypal fishing village, a cluster of houses around a carefully guarded harbour, with the Jolly Fisherman providing seafood refreshment. But there is more than meets the eye. Opposite the pub is Robson's smokehouse, which has been preparing kippers since 1856. The world famous Craster kipper, slow cured over whitewood shavings and oak chippings, has a distinctive flavour and although the herring is no longer caught locally, such is the individuality in preparation that the EU is allowing it, like champagne and Parma ham, to maintain its unique appellation. Craster's original prosperity was as a port to ship the local whinstone which, among other uses, kerbed the streets of London. But now the boats have gone and the quarry is a car park for tourists.

The coastline path threads its way between the sea breaking on the rocks and the would-be Tigers hacking the fairways on the right, passing through the village of Boulmer and the town of Alnmouth to Warkworth, the end of our, and Oswald's, seaside excursion. There are at least three points of interest on route. The first is Cullernose Point, a projection of the Whin Sill into the North Sea. From a rock-climbing point of view, this is the nearest Northumberland gets to the cliffs of the South West of England where, at high tide, you have to abseil into position to complete the routes. When I climbed there half a century ago, we always had the crag to ourselves and, as we had no access to guidebook information, assumed much of what we did might well have been new. In fact the ubiquitous Peter Biven, then stationed at RAF Boulmer, had already done all that was worth doing and our inventive naming of parts has been consigned to the waste bin of history. Nevertheless, as the only other Northumbrian crag we climbed on was Crag Lough, it was a pleasing thought that this was in effect part of the same cliff, reappearing like a leviathan some fifty miles away.

The second curiosity is the Bathing House, not far from Howick. It is an eighteenth-century cottage with steps that lead down to a carved-out rock pool. It was the property of the Grey family, who lived at Howick Hall and used the facility for their early morning dip. The family's most illustrious member was Charles, second Earl Grey, Prime Minister from 1830–1834. It is interesting to speculate whether, when reclining in his home-made jaccuzi, the 1832 constitutional reform or the blending of the tea that bears his name was uppermost in his thoughts.

The third and final curiosity to catch my eye were the various pill boxes and tank traps scattered along this section. Designed to repel the Germans in the Second World War, they remain a brooding reminder that trouble has never been far away along this stretch of England's coastline.

From Alnmouth, we round the sweep of its bay to our final castle at Warkworth. This, probably the best of our strongholds, was occupied by the Percies.

It stands four-square astride the town, a 'worm-eaten hold of ragged stone' peering down the main street from its elevated perch. Shakespeare, in his efforts to discredit Northumberland, does the building a disservice. Even today, much is intact and the keep is a fine example of medieval architecture which at the time, with its elaborate contrivances to gather water and flush out human waste, must have been regarded as state of the art. From the top of its watchtower, you can fully understand the castle's strategic positioning. Much of the ground that you have covered and are now about to cross is visible, from Cheviot to the sea, then west into central Northumberland, our next port of call.

As you'll recall, we've been relying over the past few miles on the good offices of St Oswald and, as the combined efforts of fellows saints and the Northumbrian Tourist Board have now petered out, it is only polite that we make our introductions to this continuously dependable guide. As son of Aethelfrith, King of Bernicia, and Acha, heiress of the neighbouring kingdom of Deira, he was in line to inherit all of eastern England from the Tweed to the Humber. But stability was rarely the order of the day and in 616 Aethelfrith was murdered by his brother-in-law Edwin, whereupon Oswald, realising

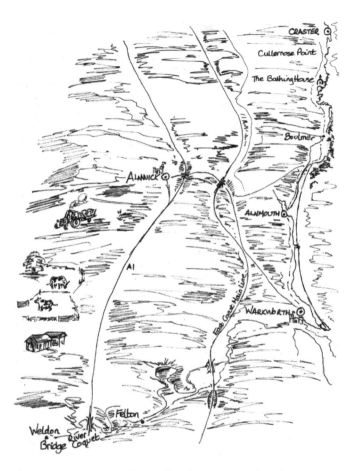

that nepotism might well take a turn for the worse, decided to beat a hasty retreat to Iona. Edwin, inevitably, got his comeuppance at the combined hands of Gwynedd and Mercia, allowing Oswald, to return, defeat the oppressors at Heavenfield and reclaim his rightful inheritance.

After this success Oswald, with a mixture of new-found piety and wit, established a period of prosperity and peace and Bede wrote him up as the ideal Christian king. Sad to say, Oswald did not live to savour the fruits of his labour. While rampaging around Mid Wales (so much for Bede's eulogy) he was defeated by the old Gwynedd–Mercia axis, whereafter his body was hacked into several fragments. It fell to his brother to pick up the pieces, which included Oswald's head and setting up the Whitby conversazione, leaving Oswald's faithful raven to lay claim to an arm which it carried around the countryside, causing the miraculous appearance of Holy Wells and Trees wherever it chanced to alight.

It is now easy enough to follow the waymarks of the late king's necromantic messenger along the banks of the river Coquet to Rothbury. The first village is Felton, once on the old A1, now like Belford a sleepy ox-bow bypassed by the new dual carriageway. It was here on an early reconnaissance that I realised how my memory had faded. I had not forgotten how friendly the folk from the North East were but, rather, *how* friendly they actually were. One of the problems of planning this route was that from time to time I needed to leave a car at my eventual destination, but was then faced with the difficulty of reaching my starting point without spending most of the day in the clutches of the public transport system. I enquired from the landlord of the Stag's Head the timetable of buses from Felton to Morpeth and, as I explained my reasons, his forehead puckered into a frown. 'I divna get the problem. Just leave yer car here and I'll tak ye where you want to gan.' The man was a complete stranger. The pub has now changed hands but the new landlord seems equally amenable and intends to build bunk-bed accommodation to sleep forty and offer the appropriate assortment of food and drink to passing walkers and cyclists.

I said the walk followed the banks of the Coquet but that was more poetic licence than topographical accuracy. Once Warkworth has been left, the route diverts along ancient green lanes once wide enough to accommodate a horse and cart, but now so overgrown that at times it is little more than a single-file path. At one stage we re-cross the main railway line and realise that, after many miles of walking east, at last we are westering home. On this occasion there is no need to risk life and limb as the trains pass overhead and, as my exploration had been conducted on a rare scorching day, I was glad to rest in the shade of the bridge. Affixed was the usual notice that in the case of damage caused by vehicular collision such and such a number should be rung. As the only vehicle capable of reaching this spot would be a quad bike, it did cross my mind that the chances of monumental contamination would be strictly limited. Still, I suppose British Rail must take into account the possibility of a particularly determined tank.

Eventually you reach Felton and cross the bridge to the north bank of the Coquet. The village has had a mixed history. In 1216 the Northern Barons chose it as a venue to complain about the tax system and, as an act of defiance, side with Alexander, King of Scotland. King John of England promptly had the place burnt down. The inhabitants, however, must have learned their lesson for, against the grain of local Jacobite support, they welcomed the Duke of Cumberland on his way to Culloden. The section from Felton to Weldon Bridge runs close to the river but, such is the steepness of the wooded gorge through which it flows, little of its course is to be seen. This inaccessibility induced an abundance of wildlife, with the otters now locked in fierce competition with the visiting fishermen from the neighbouring Angler's Arms.

At last, the riverside walk, despite cutting many corners, becomes a little closer to what it implies. It starts with a pleasant wooded stroll and later gets near enough to the water to glimpse the restored Norman church at Brinkburn Priory. It continues through the settlements at Middleheugh, Thorneyhaugh and West Raw, heading for Wagtail Farm, with fine views of Simonside and, on the opposite bank, the Cragside estate, home of the Armstrong family. The North East seems to be slow to reject feudalism and from Harry Hotspur to Sir John Hall has embraced the concept of success founded on a forceful individual surrounded by his faithful retinue. William Armstrong was such a personage. A lawyer by trade and engineer by inclination, he made his reputation through the invention of the hydraulic crane and his money out of weapons of mass destruction. Once he had persuaded the authorities to build a swing bridge over the Tyne to allow a more substantial passage to his shipyards at Elswick, the money poured in and he could devote his energies to more leisurely pursuits.

Spurred on by the memory of his childhood haunts at Rothbury, he purchased a dilapidated estate on the banks of the Coquet and, under the guidance of the architect Richard Shaw, set about creating an establishment to match his position. This was the

first private residence to use hydraulic power to drive labour-saving devices such as laundry machines, a rotisserie and eventually a dynamo to illuminate the whole house with electric light. Such was the splendour of this fairy-tale mansion that when, in 1884, the Prince and Princess of Wales made an official visit to the North East, they travelled by train to Rothbury and stayed three nights at Cragside.

It is along this same, but now disused, railway that we finally make our way, first to Wagtail Farm and then to Rothbury. Soon the town and its river are left behind and St Oswald can lengthen his stride across the moorland of the Simonside Hills, pausing only to admire the view from the particularly fine vantage points of the Iron Age Fort at Lordenshaws and Coquet Cairn, the highest point on his Way. But the good Oz would be surprised to find his route descending into a forest of conifers. Although Harwood Forest is part of the general evergreen blight, I saw signs that it is being managed to create broadleaf woodland as a habitat for red squirrels, roe deer and various birds of prey, and as our route is never far from the edges, it makes the journey considerably less claustrophobic than in many such places. Eventually the forest tracks lead to the secluded and no doubt much sought after hamlet of Harwood.

But now the downside of the original decision to avoid Kielder Forest and choose the current perambulations around the castles and coves of

Northumberland has eventually come home to roost. The land from Harwood to Hexham, despite the alliterative suggestion, cannot be described as high. This is lowland, populated not by hardy Cheviot sheep sprinkled with the occasional goat but pasture inhabited by cows. Most cows of my experience are quite happy to stand up and chew or, having chewed, lie down. Northumbrian beasts seem to incline towards a more independent spirit. Here cows will single you out like the pub bore who in return for telling you (several times over) his life story becomes somewhat obstreperous if you don't buy him a drink. If in sufficient numbers, they surround you with an air of passive but stoic aggression. To add to this general mêlée, farmers tend to leave their bulls around in what can only be described as an apparently haphazard manner, but inevitably slap across the right of way.

The route connects the villages and hamlets of Harwood, Knowesgate, Kirkwhelpington, Great and Little Bavington and Great Whittington, where the Queen's Head, the last pub on the route, often hosts the celebrations of those who have completed St Oswald's Way. The Way then continues south until it joins a section of Hadrian's Wall. Throughout, the going is much of a muchness, a series of field paths interspersed with sections of quiet country lanes. It is pleasant enough without being overexciting. In theory, there are several points of interest. An Iron Age fort, what was probably a bastle house at Catcherside and the site of a medieval village near Clarewood are all on the route. But the ravages of time have left little discernible to the uninformed eye, which tends to restrain the racing of the pulse.

More obvious, and therefore of more potential interest, are the various forms of travel that once criss-crossed this area. First, as you are approaching Knowesgate, you reach the erstwhile track of the Wansbeck Valley Railway. Built in the middle of the nineteenth century, it ran from Morpeth to Redesdale. The 'Wannie Line' at this point connected with the trains from Hexham to offer an alternative route into Scotland. A little further south, there are wide-grooved hollows made by livestock as they were driven along one of the drove roads between Scotland and England. Further south still, St Oswald's Way first crosses the Devil's Causeway, a Roman road, then joins Hadrian's Wall, now lying under the Military Road built as a result of General Wade's failure to move his troops with sufficient speed to intercept an army led by Bonnie Prince Charlie. Yet, even with this underlying history, the scenery is less engaging than the cows.

We are now walking with the general flow from Wallsend (which, for reasons best known to them, most people regard as the Wallstart) and, as the Italian job has been subsumed by the efforts of the General, are reduced to travelling immediately alongside the B6318. In effect, narrow strips of land have been given over to the Wall Walk, at times bordering the very distinctive North Ditch, thus avoiding the previous detour via Corbridge and Hexham. The end of St Oswald's Way is soon reached at Heavenfield, marked by a large wooden cross, a commemorative church and a teashop. It was here that Oswald avenged the death of his stepbrother Eanfrith at the hands of Cadwallon, the leader of the Britons.

The Tyne lies immediately below us and there are two ways to reach a convenient crossing point. First, at Heavenfield, you can take a gated lane through Fallowfield and Acomb. The alternative is to follow Hadrian's footsteps for refreshment at his eponymous pub in the unimaginatively named village of Wall, then work back east to Fallowfield and join the original suggestion. The first is shorter, but the detour is worth considering. At Planetrees, Hadrian and Wade part company and the remains once more come to the surface. In particular, a visit to Brunton Turret, one of the best preserved of such fortifications,

makes a fitting farewell before we continue south and take our leave of the Northern Marches.

South of the Tyne is the market town of Hexham, centred around the monastery built in 674 by St Wilfred. The subsequent abbey dates from the eleventh century, with substantial additions in the nineteenth; as you would expect, much of the original stone came from neighbouring Roman ruins. But this is by no means the only bit of antiquity in the town. The Old Gaol constructed in the 1330s is possibly the first purpose-built penitentiary in England. This construction must mark a step up in the process of dealing with crime. Under Anglo Saxon law there were only three remedies: death, mutilation and fine. The first two speak for themselves; the latter meant the confiscation of the criminal object, such as the sword that illegally inflicted the wound. Interestingly enough, this tit-for-tat remedy remained part of English Common Law until some unfortunate was involved in a railway accident and attempted to sequestrate the offending locomotive.

The other claim to fame in these parts is the Hexham Riot. This arose out of the change in the method of conscription into the local militia. Up to 1761 the practice had been that the local dignitaries picked those who should fill the draft, but then someone, in whatever passed for Whitehall at the time, decided that the conscripts should be chosen by lot. The outcome was much protest and fifty-one killed by the North Yorkshire Militia. I can see the protesters' point of view. No doubt the local ne'er-do-wells were first on the squire's hit list, whilst the more worthy were deservedly spared.

As Hexham hoves into view, and as we are reaching the end of our journey through the county and people of Northumberland, it is worth considering actually who or what is a Geordie. There are those who feel that there should be some identifiable geographical element, as in the case of Bow Bells. This would define their master race, enabling the true Geordie to ignore the rest of Northumberland and rely on the Angel of the North, another St Peter at the Gate, to keep unwanted southerners at bay. A traditional definition was to be born within scent of the Tyne but, such was the pollution in the Fifties and Sixties, the constituency would have spread from the Scottish Borders to Robin Hood's Bay, so the suggestion was quietly dropped. To be fair, the waters have now been sufficiently cleansed that the Tyne is one of the better salmon rivers in England. The probable truth of the origin of the term is less romantic. Much to the derision of the rest of the North East, the not-so-good burghers of Newcastle decided for commercial reasons to support the Hanoverian King

George against the Jacobite uprising, which act of sycophancy earned them their dismissive nickname. An equally plausible reason is that the local miners preferred the safety lamp invented by George Stevenson to the more commonly used Davy lamp. In fact the corruption 'divvy' still means someone who is pretty slow on the uptake and of no particular use.

But, for rest of the country, 'Geordie' tends to mean anyone born or living between the Tees and the Tweed, and although this would bring cries of protest from the County Palatinate of Durham, there is some logic behind the assumption. Even today it does seem a land apart, characterised by its often impenetrable language. Neither the Scots to the north nor the Vikings to the south decided to settle permanently and although the Normans went in for their usual harrying, even they decided, unless matters got too out of hand, to let sleeping dogs lie. So for practical purposes, once the legions had left, very little changed and something of a timewarp set in.

It was this Roman withdrawal that had caused resident Celts a bit of a headache. Fearing an invasion by the Picts, they decided to hire mercenaries, a mixture of Angles and Saxons, to guard their northern borders. They were, however, soon to regret their decision as word got around that Britain was a good place to live and the Anglo-Saxons arrived in force. Soon the locals were driven out to the margins and an Anglo- or Eng-land was established where Anglo-Saxon rule and, more importantly, language prevailed. Eventually it became the turn of the invaders to bend the knee. First incursions were made by the Danes and finally the Norman conquest generally reduced not only them and but also their language to a subordinate role.

That is, everywhere but in the North East. It has been estimated that nowadays only thirty percent of the language in general use stems from Anglo-Saxon English. In Northumbria it is eighty percent. The Geordie accent often accurately represents the original 'English' vocabulary, as in 'coo' for 'cow' or 'hoos' for 'house'. Even apparent confusions such as 'aarl larn yew' for 'I'll teach you' are often technically correct English. In this case, the Angle word for 'teach' is in fact 'learan'. There is much talk in certain quarters about the maintenance of Proper English, but if you want to hear English spoken properly you can do worse than 'gan an tak yersel te Snods Edge, man' (seize the opportunity to visit those who live in the vicinity of Winter's Hill).

The various transgressions of the Reivers and their kind, together with a bitter east wind, meant that the area did not figure too high on a list of ideal retirement homes. Few people moved in and those that did were generally sent up from London to sort things out. Among these law-enforcers was the Percy family. Descended from Danish raiders who settled in the Norman Pays de Caux, they had been rewarded with bits of Yorkshire for their part in the invasion but were soon appointed Warden of the Marches and settled in Northumberland. At a later date, for another part in helping depose Richard II and placing Henry Bolingbroke, Duke of Lancaster, on the throne, they were rewarded with the title of Earl and, in 1766, Duke of Northumberland.

The epitome of the Geordie spirit was encapsulated in the vaulting ambition of Harry Hotspur, son of Northumberland, and this in turn was captured by Shakespeare in his play *Henry IV* (Part1). The Percies felt that their part in the promotion of Bolingbroke to king had been less than appreciated, with promises broken and favours unrewarded, and as a result Hotspur declined to surrender his Scottish prisoners to the King. Despite various attempts to offer him a compromise, Hotspur whose 'blood more stirs to rouse a lion than start a hare' would have none of it and, inevitably, let down by his supposed allies, he dies a heroic but pointless death at the hands of the King's apparently wayward son. The modern-day inheritors of Hotspur's attitude are some of the local football supporters who would rather their team lose 4–5 than gain a 1–0 victory by boring the opposition to death, and they too, when humiliation stares them in the face, can only echo Hotspur's dying words:

I better brook the loss of brittle life
Than those proud titles thou hast won of me;
They wound my thoughts worse than thy sword
    my flesh.

To anyone who regards this connection as rather fanciful, I would point out that the Robsons, Milburns and Charltons were amongst the more ferocious of the Reiver families.

—4—

Where the tough get going
Hexham to Tan Hill

One of the problems with a walk of this nature is that at some stage or another you are bound to go through a concentration of houses. Going to towns, or even being in towns, is not a problem. In fact, if you have run out of money, calories or steam it can be a positive godsend. The North of England, if not like the Scottish Highlands where you pass a pub or petrol station at your peril, can have remote stretches and it is wise to take stock while you can. Whether it is necessary to go as far as Wainwright's apostrophe on entering Middleton-in-Teesdale

Here are beds and breakfasts, pretty girls, fish and
chips, beer, ice-cream. Yippee!

is a matter of taste. Suffice to say that Hexham has its moments.

The problem is not entry but exit. I knew from my reading of the map that if I could reach Greenridge Farm I would have access to the Hexham Moors, but the way out is not only uphill but also pretty densely populated. As I had written in Volume I about the pleasures of wandering around housing estates, and

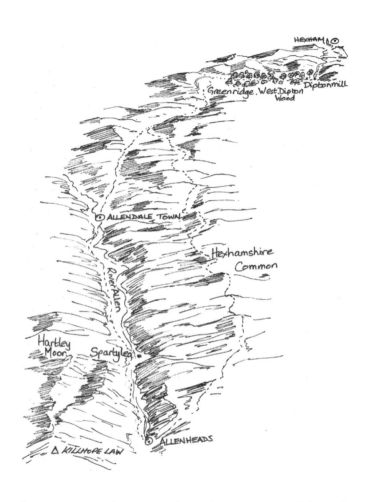

having no wish to wax lyrical once more, I hoped
to find a more subtle way to bypass the general

populace. My original idea had been to make my way to Hexham Racecourse, striking a path through the strip of woodland that encloses West Dipton Burn as far west as possible. But chance moves in mysterious ways. Unable to stride out along the route of choice (a leg infection had reduced me to stumbling around supported by a stick) I decided to use the enforced rest to examine the area more closely. I noticed that, virtually from the town centre, there is a connection of footpaths that leads to Hole House at the eastern, or, as I thought, wrong end of the wood. A path then leads to Diptonmill. Here lies treasure indeed. The Dipton Mill Inn is described by the author of *Fifty Favourite Northumberland Pubs* as 'probably the smallest pub in the county and serves a choice of real ales made by the landlord in his own micro-brewery'. This description hints at but also understates the truth. It is a gem. In every respect, externally and internally, it is a proper pub. If you don't understand what that means, then no further explanation will help.

If you have passed at a suitable moment, for as well as being a proper pub, it has also proper opening hours, you can continue through Dipton Wood fortified by such delights as Shire Bitter or Whapweasel. The woods in no way form an anticlimax to the happy hour and offer a delightful stroll as far as an open stretch of meadow. There are now two ways: the low road and the high road. The former passes beneath Cats Crag and Queen's Cave where, whatever history says, legend has it that after the battle of Hexham Queen Margaret of Anjou was attacked by a robber. But, as the path had already disappeared into the stream, with resultant scrabbling along the bank side, I chose the latter. This more or less follows the boundary wall but rather lands you in the long grass until both options reconnect and you can burst onto a lane just south of Nubbock Lodge. Here, half a mile of roadwork brings you to the desired cluster of buildings at Greenridge. A bridleway is joined that marches doggedly and directly towards Allendale Town, while road (and at one time rail) had to skulk around the foothills to reach the same destination. Do not be tempted by well-made tracks that cross the route. They are for shooters not walkers, as once more we are entering serious grouse country.

Although it is possible to stay high until you reach Allenheads, I really wanted to drop down to Allendale Town and the valley that holds the East Allen river. My reason was threefold: for more than fifty years I had driven past signposts advertising its presence, yet had never visited the dale; it was one of the original suggestions as a route for that section of the Pennine Way, but at the time private land barred the obvious and direct access to the Wall; and I had also heard of and been intrigued by Isaac's Tea Trail which seemed both to offer a suitable way south and an opportunity to explore the area.

Isaac Holden must have been an interesting man. He had been a lead miner until cheaper Spanish imports caused havoc to the local industry. So he opened a grocer's shop in Allendale and, as a travelling salesman, hawked his tea around neighbouring farms and outlying hamlets. His patch was a circle connecting the towns and villages of Nenthead, Alston and Keenly, a distance of some thirty-six miles, providing tea, coffee and, no doubt, local news to the isolated communities that lay on the way. But he was more than a pedlar. He also sold his poems and tracts to raise money for good causes. A staunch Methodist, he raised £150 (a not inconsiderable sum at the time) to pay off the debt owed by a Wesleyan chapel, thus saving it from closure, and, encouraged by this initial triumph, further amounts to provide a freshwater supply for Allendale Town, promote a Penny Bank and found a clothing fund for poor women and children.

But the pinnacle of his success was raising sufficient money to provide a hearse. It was a matter of general concern that the dead should be treated with proper respect. However, it was often the case that to reach consecrated ground the corpse had to be stuffed into a wicker basket and carried, slung between two poles, before eventually being deposited in a coffin barrow. It was Isaac's burning ambition to offer a more dignified alternative. Encouraged by local worthies, Mathew Catcherside and Michael Swan, he commissioned 1,000 copies of a likeness of himself, photographed by William Pruddah and engraved by Mason Jackson, the celebrated Art Editor of the London Illustrated News. His intention was to sell these for sufficient coppers to buy the hearse and requisite trappings. Yet, such was his anxiety that he might fail in this project or, like Noah, be laughed at for his efforts, he kept the purpose of the sales a secret even from his wife. Eventually, on July 9th 1856, he was able to go to Newcastle with £25 10s to acquire his life's goal, which a few days later he proudly presented to the people of West Allen.

What is remarkable about the whole affair is the nature of the man himself. He was regarded as an eccentric driven by religious fervour. He had little education and was thought in many ways to be rather simple, but his drive and enthusiasm are unquestionable. He did not write well but wrote what he believed. The *North of England Advertiser* produced a piece entitled 'Eccentric Benevolence' which seems to sum up the man. After a general introduction to his life and charitable achievements, the article describes how he wrote 'what he calls a poem, which he sells in his perambulations … It is said his printer is sometimes desirous of making more improvements in the manuscript than Isaac will permit as he does not like to have too much interference with the originality of his compositions.'

His Trail starts in Allendale Town centre, an impressive market square surrounded by what once were hotels which accommodated farmers come to market and, later, Edwardian tourists. You cross the river East Allen and follow the west bank until you reach New Shield, where you cut a corner to Pry Hill. You then join the Black Way, a bridlepath that leads over the moors to Nenthead, but before reaching Philipson's Fold swing off left and make your way back to the river, knowing that rest is at hand. Your companion, a man dressed in sombre black weighed down by his pedlar's burden still has a long way to go and, having paused to readjust the straps of his pack, plods on. The final stretch into Allenheads is a pleasant walk on a late summer's evening during which you can dry out from the effects of any earlier showers.

Always provided, you, unlike the author, manage to look where you are going and not step off the bank into the racing stream. Wet or dry, the Allenheads Inn is a welcome sight and fully repays your efforts to get there. It merits another muted paean from the author of the Favourite Fifty: 'a comfortable bar with a log fire and bookshelves'—and that delightful rarity, a Residents' Lounge.

Now after some 200 miles and the better part of two weeks' walking you are about to leave Northumberland and enter Durham, once the county of mines and miners. If the words 'mines' and 'Durham' appear in the same sentence, most people would assume that the material being extracted was coal. That was not the case in 'them there hills' we are about to cross. There, the mining produced lead. As a non-corrosive metal it had always had its uses, but once the Industrial Revolution got under way, the demand escalated and in the eighteenth and nineteenth centuries the landowners who ran the mines made a serious amount of money. So much so that the Blackett-Beaumont family who owned the estates around Allenheads were thought to be the richest commoners in England.

But the few making a fortune at the expense of the many was commonplace in Victorian England and in itself is not that worthy of investigation. What is interesting is the process that produced this particular wealth. Or, to put it another way, why did these miners put up with the inhospitable surroundings of the bleak upland moors and not drift down to an easier life on the coast and mine the coal that paid better wages? The answer lies in the quality of their way of life. Extracting lead had happened from time immemorial, using a hush or torrent of water to expose the location of the vein. Such a method was haphazard and could not be relied upon to sustain a family. As a result, miners from these parts were also farmers and spent their time between the two occupations. The staple was the three Ps—pigs, poultry and potatoes—rather than the hope of striking rich.

Consequently there were no set shifts, no formal clocking on and off, and the miners came and went as circumstance dictated. In fact, the only strike that ever occurred in the district was when one mine manager insisted that there should be an eight-hour day. In addition, rather than being seen as a dull repetitive task, lead mining had its own edge. Groups of miners formed themselves into partnerships and bargained with the owner's agents on a price for the job. The partnership agreed to be paid at a fixed rate for the amount of ore extracted. If the vein turned out to be of a higher quality than expected, the miners would cash in. If the dross outweighed the ore, they had to suffer for their collective lack of judgement.

The management soon realised that a contented workforce was a good workforce and spent much time improving the general lot. Schools were built and the exploitation of child labour was, unlike in the coal mines and cotton mills, kept to such a minimum that a member of an official Commission was able to report in 1842 that the population of the dales was 'as well educated and of intellectual capacity and acquirement surpassing any I have met with in England'. Perhaps most of all, men stayed because the work had an intrinsic interest. Various additional metals were found in the process of digging out the lead and had to be identified and, if of sufficient value, separately dealt with. It would be an oversimplification to say that coal mining was nothing more than hacking out, dragging off and throwing the result on the fire, but it did not have an end product which the miner could see and have reason to believe would continue to exist after his time was past.

Leaving Allenheads, you return to the bridge at Dirt Pot and set off up the Carriers' Way which leads over to Killhope lead mine. The carriers were the packhorses bearing the lead ore to the smelt mill at Allenheads, so the path is both obvious and at a reasonable incline. Progress is swift and by using a bulldozed track to a shooting lodge you are quickly at the top of the first objective, Killhope Law. Even in the thickest of mists you will know when you have arrived. The summit is cluttered with not only a trig point and an unusually large cairn but also a thirty-foot mast. Assuming vision, the views back into Allendale are idyllic, green fields and grassy knolls, wooded rifts and vales with streams and brooks, no doubt, purling and babbling in the approved manner. Take a good look. You will not, for many a mile, see their like again.

Once Northumberland is left, you are about to cross some of the wildest country I have experienced in these isles. I suggested in my introduction to Volume I that when the going gets tough, the North gets going. There is a corollary to that proposition. When the North gets tough, the Durham Moors get going. Regardless of where the County Commissioners place their boundary lines, there are certain areas that categorically belong to themselves and the stretch of country running along the Durham–Cumbria border between Killhope Law and Tan Hill is one of them.

After the Allenheads Inn you will find little in the way of sustenance other than the occasional patch of cloudberries until you reach Tan Hill. In fact, the Langdon Beck Hotel is the sole form of organised shelter and provender to be found en route. The moors are also a lonely place. I must have spent a dozen separate days wandering around the area looking at a variety of possibilities. During that time I saw no one other than the proverbial one man and his dog. What is more, apart from the extremely busy A66, you cross only three relatively minor roads. Even there, not a sign of a parked car to indicate others are somewhere on the hill. If anything goes wrong, Samaritans of any moral persuasion are in short supply. Traditionally, this was the normal circumstance of travel, but to those more accustomed to be waited on by service stations and travel lodges, it could come as a bit of a shock.

At a good bit more than forty miles, with only one stopping place, it is a pretty decent stretch for the legs. But it would be a mistake to assume the distance shown on the map is a true measure. Once more we are in the country of the blanket bog but, unlike the Forest of Bowland, it is not hemmed with its 'Hornby Road' to allow an alternative easy thoroughfare. In the main, it is boot-sucking peat that sprouts extremely tenacious heather. From time to time an inviting green strip appears as a bowling green surface that will at last allow you to make decent progress. But this is fool's gold. The lush greenery is the surface of marsh so deep and intractable that horses have been swallowed up without trace. As a result, with all the meanderings necessary to avoid these pitfalls you can sensibly double the apparent distance calculated with a bit of string. There are many ways you might come to a sticky end on the Durham Moors but take heart, being run over probably isn't one of them.

The first section, from Killhope Law to Killhope Cross, the highest point on a classified road in England, is a good example of what is to come. On the map it looks of little consequence. A mile or so of land sloping gently down from the summit towards the A689. The obvious line seems to be the Northumberland–Durham border until it bumps into Cumbria, then turns sharp south to the road. Nothing could be more simple. In reality, it is anything but. The initial downward slope presents few problems but once the land starts to level out everything changes. The ditch that marks the border disappears into a semi-subterranean maze of peat groughs and hags, each with its own particularly extensive green bog.

During this slow motion helter-skelter, your head from time to time appears above the surface of the wilderness, giving you a brief opportunity to pinpoint your position. Bog-avoidance has made that carefully prepared compass bearing irrelevant and, as the ground dips, you plunge once more into the depths, hoping you are moving in approximately the right direction. No sign of a path or anything approaching a path. Occasionally, there are the tracks of a quad bike but you soon learn to ignore them when you discover these machines are designed to skim over ground into which you immediately sink. You are in a no man's land, or rather an everyman's land, as you are never quite certain whether at any point in time or place your feet are in Northumberland, Durham or Cumbria. Your Satnav becomes the distant roar of the motorbike engines as these devotees of steep inclines and dangerous bends roar over the tarmac that is your eventual goal.

I think it is fair to say that this stretch is as bad as it gets. Or at least so it seemed to me, though I might have been too complacent and taken insufficient care before I left Killhope Law, but even if I have been overestimating the difficulties, it is probably wise to heed the words of Paddy Dillon, a man not given to hyperbole. He states in his guide to *Walking in the North Pennines*: 'This can be very difficult country in bad weather.'

After you have reached the road, matters become more straightforward. Although the conditions underfoot are similar, navigation becomes easier. In contrast to the Northumberland–Durham border, the frontier between Durham and Cumbria is clearly defined for most of the journey and, although insufficient feet have passed to form a path, the heather gives the impression of being downtrodden or, more probably, downcast at being thwarted in its role as an impromptu ambuscade. The way to our next County Top, Burnhope Seat, even has first a fence and then a wall to guide us and, given good visibility, you are kept on course over Nag's Head and Dead Stones by a particularly large cairn on the summit of the latter. In poor weather, hang onto the fence and follow the watershed until the former high point of County Durham is reached. As you pull up the final slopes, the top of some odd-looking ironwork pokes its head over the skyline. An entrepreneur, in a flourish of hope over experience, has erected ski tows. Welcome to the St Moritz of the Durham Moors.

For those who like to be precise, the summit cairn of Burnhope Seat is actually not the highest point in the former county. The old boundary passed to the east of the summit, so the highest point in old Durham is somewhere amongst a squadgy mess a little lower to your left and of course, being half way up a slope, cannot really be called a top at all. The highest top in what was formerly Durham, i.e. the highest point where whichever way you turn you are about to go downhill, is in fact Scaud Hill, about a mile to the east of your present position. If a stickler for accuracy, you could easily enough include it in your descent. If a pragmatist, you will just bash on down until you reach the second road crossing, at Swallow Hole on the B6277.

Here, *mirabile dictu*, you will find a miners' track to take you to Cow Green Reservoir. Cherish the moment when you can take your eyes from your feet and stride out with a confidence born of the knowledge that the next unguarded step will not plunge you thigh-deep into the morass. As you are able to inspect your surroundings, it now becomes obvious why the planners built where they did. The reservoir lies in a bowl bounded by the Pennine heights that culminate in Cross Fell. The Tees rises at this point, a barely discernible trickle but, with feeding streams adding to its strength and energy supplied by cataracts and waterfalls, it eventually spreads into a broad brown river that flows into the sea. In fact, the ground that you have just covered is the gathering ground for all the local waterways. When you stood on Burnhope Seat, the source of the South Tyne lay to your west and the Wear to the east. They are all mighty rivers but, of the three, the Wear has my affection, wending its way seawards past those other county tops of Durham Cathedral and the Stadium of Light to the place of my childhood. One day I must follow its meanders but for the moment Mickle Fell looms, both to the eye and in the mind.

The crossing of Mickle Fell, formerly the high point of Yorkshire but now safely ensconced within the boundary of Durham, is the crux of the whole journey. This is the only occasion where factors other than personal determination come into play. The land you have to traverse is a military firing range and for many years the summit was officially out of bounds. More tolerant days have established a truce and there are days when the red flag is not flying and access is allowed. Any continuous journey has to be planned around these dates. In fact the land we cross is on the very edge of the range and local shepherds and gamekeepers seem regularly to go about their business with a certain casual aplomb. The normal practice, according to one veteran, was that if you heard a funny noise you should 'hoik yorsel' into the nearest dike.

The fell also had its natural defences. Maize Beck

to the north and Connypot Beck to the south. Both have to be forded if a direct line is to be taken and the former, when it rushes to join the foaming Tees before plunging over the waterfall at High Force, can be a very difficult proposition and it may be necessary to follow the Pennine Way almost as far as High Cup Nick until a newly constructed bridge allows access to the other bank. But there is a plus side if you can make the more direct crossing. A line of boundary stones leads up the hill, thereafter continuing up hill and down dale along your future direction of travel. They are also numbered in descending order until finally, somewhere in the middle of nowhere (aka Stainmore), even they give up the ghost. Not all the stones are still in place. Some have been removed for other purposes, some have simply sunk. In the beginning, it's quite fun trying to spot the next one, then trying to decipher the weather-beaten number, but after you've stepped more than once through the crust of a sphagnum moss pool the novelty starts to wear off.

But I am getting ahead of myself. You are still standing on the B6277 at Swallow Hole. This large depression is a shake hole. These cavities are caused by a land fall or slip beneath the surface and the area is peppered with them. They are clearly marked on the map and care should be taken in their vicinity, otherwise the likes of Swallow Hole might have a slightly different spelling. All around you is now designated as an Area of Outstanding Natural Beauty and, with 772 square miles, is the largest of its type. Nature lovers and particularly botanists make the long journey to see and photograph species unique to this area (curiously some varieties flourish because of the toxic waste caused by lead mining) and, when you get there, the talk in the bar of the Langdon Beck Hotel is as much about spring gentians and birdseye primroses, otters and eagle owls as it is as about sterling feats on the nearby Pennine Way.

Assuming you spent the night at the hotel, you now have to retrace your steps to the reservoir where service roads lead to the top of Cauldron Snout, or, better still, make a short diversion and join the Pennine Way further downstream and, approaching from the east, skirt Falcon Clints before clambering up alongside the impressive cascade. From the top of the Snout, continue on the Way until it is possible to cross Maize Beck and begin the ascent of Mickle Fell. The route makes height in a sedate fashion before the hill rears its head for the final 300 feet. Once the summit plateau is reached, there is a short stroll to the cairn where you can look around and get your bearings. If it weren't for the man-made reservoir at Cow Green, you could be anywhere. In every direction, the miles of virtually uninhabited land roll away to the horizon. The sense of remoteness the view gave me was akin to standing on the top of A'Mhaighdean— and A'Mhaighdean has been described as 'that most un-get-at-able of all hills' in Britain. The descent to King's Pot is steeper but after that the land flattens and works its way via Hanging Seal and Connypot Beck to the cattle grid that bestrides the highest point of the B6276.

Cross the road and continue to follow the boundary stones over Dow Crag and Benty Hill to Pind Hill. Here is the hinge of the expedition. Any shelter is still some distance away but there is a choice. You can press on through the bog to Tan Hill or, if tiring of that particular delight, swing east to reach habitation in Baldersdale. The direct route is shorter but probably not that much quicker and involves following the county boundary over Round Hill, Great Dodd and Bedloo Hill until you reach the busy A66, and then, after with some considerable care crossing the tarmac, continue in the same line until Tan Hill is reached. The alternative is to abandon the moor and follow what, in its beginnings, the map marks rather optimistically as a bridleway, running

parallel to Balder Beck, until it develops into a more
discernible track. This in turn joins a minor road that
intercepts the Pennine Way. If enough is enough, you

can break your journey here. If you are still raring to go, it is only another ten miles to Tan Hill.

I would and did choose the Baldersdale alternative with its passage under rather than across the A66, but there was probably more than a rational explanation behind my decision. It may have been something to do with my experience of walking the land between the B6276 and the A66. I had, on several occasions, approached Pind Hill, each time from a different direction, and had invariably brought bad weather with me. My abiding memory is a head-down plodge, seeing nothing but sheep, those silent observers of human folly, who balefully watched my stuttering progress. The more I walked, the more a repetitive rhythm began to fill my mind. I eventually recognised the tempo as Lewis Carroll's nonsense poem 'Jabberwocky': 'Twas brillig and the slithy toves / Did gyre and gimble in the wabe / All mimsy were the borogroves', etc.

I could not rid my mind of the incessant beat and, as I walked, started to fit in words of my own: 'Twas Sunday and the skulken peat / Did glot and gluer in its bed.' For those who might be interested in plodding verse, its entirety appends this chapter. I also recalled that Robert Graves, in his autobiography *Goodbye to All That*, suffered a similar affliction when trying to cope with the rigours and horror of war in the trenches. Although he found it irritating, it paradoxically seemed to offer some sort of solace. By the time I had reached Pind Hill in pouring rain for the fourth time, I began to realise the educational method that lay behind the apparent military madness inflicted on me by the CCF those many years ago. Or, to quote Edgar's rather gloomy form of optimism in *King Lear*, 'the worst is not / So long as we can say, "This is the worst."'

O Frabjous Joy

'Twas Sunday and the skulken peat
Did glot and gluer in its bed
All sodden were the aching feet
And the last can was dead.

Beware the Durham Moors, my son
With bogs that suck and lings that snatch
Beware the shak-hole traps and shun
That lustish greener patch.
He took his trekking poles in hand
For long the distant foe he'd sought

A can he hid by the cattle grid
And chortled at the thought.
Yet, as in slurish mud he stood
And listened to the curlew's call
That creekoch cry that bodes no good
The rain began to fall.
One two! One two! No time to mope
The trekking poles went slick and slack
He'd reached the cairn, now full of hope
He turned, salumphing, back.
But can was gone, the thief away
No point in either rant or shout.
Of hope, The Arms the only ray
But even there the lights were out.

'Twas Sunday and the skulken peat
Did glot and gluer in its bed
All sodden were the aching feet
And the last can was dead.

— 5 —

Up hill and down dale
Tan Hill to Kettlewell

At 1,732 feet, the Tan Hill Inn is the highest of England's licensed premises, first mentioned in 1586 by William Camden in his county-by-county topographical description, *Britannia*. It was also the subject of a boundary dispute. As a result of the changes in 1974, it was deemed to have moved into Durham but this caused such an outrage amongst Yorkshiremen that they instigated a review which in 1987 returned the pub to its native heath. The inn's original purpose was to sustain the miners who produced the coal that fired the lime kilns at Arkengarthdale, and when the last mine shut down in 1929 it must have taken a very determined landlord to keep going in what then became an out-of-the-way location. Commercial relief arrived in 1965, when it was decided that England's first long distance footpath, the Pennine Way, should pass the front door.

The inn offers shelter, food and liquid refreshment. But transatlantic visitors should be warned that, where the cat acts as the official Vermin Control Operative and the dog claims the best seat in the house, there is little sign of heated swimming pool, saunas or room service. Habitués of the world's Sheratons will feel particularly bereft. But if you are, as is often the case, cold, wet and hungry, you may feel eternally grateful that local industry once required the provision of any service in such a remote spot.

In fact, the Pennine Wayers were not the first long distance walkers to avail themselves of the inn's existence. In 1952, to celebrate the jubilee of the Rucksack Club, the members decided to invent and complete a new non-stop hill walk. Thus was born the Tan Hill to Cat and Fiddle, a distance of around 120 miles and quite a bit of up and down, first completed by Vin Desmond in 54 hours 10 minutes. The route, although crossing over Great Shunner Fell and through Hawes, lay a little to the east of the now Pennine Way and took its course through Grassington and Todmorden until it eventually reached Marsden and joined the shared and well-established paths over Bleaklow, Kinder and Castle Naze. Nevertheless, it must have been a prototype for the official Way that was to open a decade or so later.

Moreover, the history of that now renowned Edale–Kirk Yetholm excursion had an earlier genesis. During the Second World War, a detachment of airborne troops under the command of Major David Clark was stationed in Edale for special endurance training on the surrounding moors. Realising he might instigate the fulfilment of a long-held ambition, Fred Heardman, licensee of the Nag's Head and the first man to complete the double Marsden–Edale, suggested that they should do something really challenging. His proposition was a walk that could well start in the Cheviots and finish at Edale, avoiding wherever possible all easy options. Such were the weather and terrain, it took them two days to complete the first twenty miles, whereupon Clark decided they had better make use of existing tracks. Better progress was made and after a further four days they were within a single march of completing the 250-mile slog to the Nag's Head. The War Office, however, intervened and they were withdrawn to headquarters. On 17th September they landed on other foreign fields, from which encounter many were never to return. A bridge too far, it was said. Food for thought if you plod on that well-worn way,

But, although it is never too far away, the Pennine Way is not for us and at Tan Hill we wheel sharp right and set off across the moors in the direction of Nine Standards Rigg. We are now once more in lead mining country, but a traveller of that time would have noticed certain differences from the practices further north. Knitting for profit was a traditional occupation in the Dales and the pastime was not the preserve of the female sex. Because, whatever your job, you usually had to walk some distance to work; so, to employ the time usefully, the men would knit as they went. Edward Stillman, minister of Keld, for example, continuously knitted as he walked to London in 1820 to beg funds for his parish. Miners, in particular, were 'inveterate and very swift knitters' who, when wishing to take a short rest, would sit 'for six needles'. Their products were sold at the local fairs, occasions for much frivolity and, despite the strong Nonconformist presence, heavy drinking. The whole matter throws a somewhat different light on the term 'open-cast'.

Our eighteenth-century peakbagger would have also noticed a shift in the nature of industrial relations. Whether it was a question of local temperament or geological uncertainties, they were not conducted in the same harmonious manner noted in Allendale, which had been held in the firm grip of a single landowner. One protracted dispute over the Beldi mines in Swaledale was particularly acrimonious. Parkes and Company had leased and begun to mine the Out Pasture from Thomas Smith of Crackpott

Hall. His neighbour, Lord Pomfret, claimed that the Hall Pasture was part of the wastes of the Manor of Healaugh, the mineral rights of which had been reserved to him. There was already bad blood between the two and a lengthy legal struggle commenced. Although the courts consistently found for Smith and that the pasture had 'time out of mind' been fenced

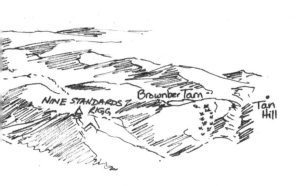

from the waste and was part of Crackpott Estate, Lord Pomfret persisted and appealed to the House of Lords on no less than three occasions. Such was the expense of these various trials, the accumulated costs eventually ruined the peer, who was incarcerated in what I assume was a better class of Debtors' Prison, the Tower of London.

During all this the miners on both sides entered into the fray with a will. Shafts were provocatively sunk in the disputed territory then, in turn, deliberately flooded to flush out the opposition. Possession of the Spout Gill Smelt Mill yo-yoed to and fro and bings of ore were stolen and reclaimed. The outcome has a somewhat modern sporting ring. Each miner espoused his owner's cause with the fervour of today's football fan, taking any slightest setback as a personal insult. Nor did the owners or their agents seem to exercise much in the way of restraint. The former were anxious to protect their profits by any means available and the latter seized the opportunity to make their fortune through dubious practices and favouring their friends. So great was the level of corruption that Lord Pomfret on one occasion expostulated that 'the only way to have a just account and make a full profit of the Estates of the mines of Swaledale is not to employ anyone as [Agent] who is a Yorkshireman'. I presume that once the dust had settled for the day, the miners would pick up their knitting and return to their villages in the valley, possibly, in their excitement, dropping a stitch or two as they went.

Although there is still evidence of these workings where mammals of all types and size have fallen forever into half-hidden holes, our journey takes a quieter route above this confusion. But quieter has its downside, particularly for the nervous. Although the compilers of the Domesday Book probably did not investigate the detail with their usual due diligence, they were not wrong to describe all the land above Reeth as a 'wasteland'. In most places on the English hills there are discernible features to guide you from one point to another. The 'wasteland' above Reeth is not one of them. Our aim is to travel from Tan Hill to Nine Standards Rigg with as little deviation or, for that matter, hesitation or repetition as possible. The compass bearing is virtually due west and a steady hand and a bit of forward planning should see you through. Mist makes a difference. First, it sets up a conflict between your finely tuned sense of direction and the apparent aberrations of the magnetic needle, a state of mind further confused by ill-digested facts about the influence of subterranean metallic deposits. Second, encouraged by the former dithering, there is a tendency to take the easiest line, which inevitably means slowly sliding downhill to find yourself in entirely the wrong valley. If in doubt, the journey can be completed in two legs by first setting a bearing for Brownber Tarn, then starting again.

To add to this general dithering, mist is always damp and usually cold and the higher you go, the worse it gets. As a result, it can become psychologically depressing. Sceptics within their log-fired living room may find it simple enough to pour scorn but when you are alone, chilled and a little bewildered by the swirlish mist, it is easy to imagine other agencies at work and start to catch the splish, splash, click, clack of Absalom 'Needles' Grimshaw as he goes about his business. So much so that tales of supernatural happenings in the mountains tend to grow like Hydra's heads. The example most often evoked in the storm-battered bothy as the roof creaks and the candles gutter is the ghost of Fear Liath Mor, the Great Grey Man of Ben Macdui. Living in the Cairngorms, a remote wilderness plateau riven with deep gashes and secret thoroughfares, the phantom, if that is what it is, has been seen, heard or imagined by an assortment of men good and true, including a forester, a couple of Buddhist monks and the President of the Alpine Club. Variously, it has been described as between six and twenty feet tall and given to 'mumbling' while eating bamboo shoots. The telling assumes even greater credibility if the story is delivered in a suitably sinister Scottish accent.

The world that occupies the space between imagination and truth is the stuff of fiction and a certain type of mountain literature is not slow to explore, or even exploit, it. Occasionally, it is for humorous effect, as in the various vertiginous meanderings of The Doctor and his entourage in G J F Dutton's *The Ridiculous Mountains*, but more often it is a springboard for the macabre. The 'whodunit', in particular, likes to cloak the dastardly deed with mists that drift tantalisingly across the reader's unravelling of the plot. *Drift, swirl, lour*—the very words applied to our mist-ridden moors give the phenomenon an animate and less than benign quality. Memories older than memory itself rise to the surface and each looming shape, so harmless in sunlight, appears as a harbinger of some indescribable threat.

It was therefore a certain relief when the latest apparition turned out to be one of the Nine Standards that were my original goal. These cairns are not the idle pursuit of holidaymakers but carefully constructed and up to ten feet high. Their manufacture or purpose is not known for certain, but one suggestion is that they were built by the Romans to give the impression of a well fortified hilltop. Tradition has it that they were built by local miners with nothing better to do, but a more likely explanation is that they marked some once-significant boundary line. As with most such matters, you can take your choice or even make up your own explanation. Anyway, it kept my mind distracted from the splash, splash, splash, click, click, click that had also stopped every time I paused to check my bearings.

You now join Wainwright's Coast to Coast, which you will follow into the town of Kirkby Stephen and, assuming you took the direct route, the first shops since Hexham. There is a bustle about the place that seems significantly different from the drips of habitation we have passed during the previous sixty or seventy miles. It's another good point to take stock, in all senses of the word. The name on the map has our next objective as Ravenstonedale but passes on the local tongue as Rizundal and we continue on the well signposted Way of Alf, under railway lines used and disused, across Smardale Fell to Smardale Bridge. Here we leave Wainwright and, turning south, follow Scandal Beck and our own initiative to cross the A685 and enter the village.

To say that Ravenstonedale is a peculiar place would, today, imply that there is something a little strange about it. Like so many words, 'peculiar' has had its meaning distorted and the original sense of 'particular' or 'special' has been overtaken by the alternatives of 'odd' or 'not quite right'. I am using the term as a compliment, for Ravensdale appears to exist and to have always existed in its own enclosed and particular world. In 1877, the Revd William Nichols in a lecture on the history and traditions of the village stated, 'Happily we are aside from the tourists' route and this saves us from the vulgarisation of the quiet of our noble hills' and Thomas Whitehead, as late as 1932, described the place: 'Isolated, remote, unseen either from the main roads or from the railways, one can easily understand how, in the Tudor and early Stuart Periods, this small hamlet would be a self-contained community.' Today, still sheltered from the hum of the traffic bearing down on the M6, little seems to have changed during the intervening years.

Yet, there are peculiarities in both senses of the word. The first is its name. There is no river Raven to explain the name of the dale and although a Raven Brook was eventually christened, this was probably based more on romantic expectation than historical fact. The more likely explanation is that it is a corruption of *Rabenstein*, the German term for a place of public execution, and the existence of the nearby Gallows Hill, which we shall pass on our way to Sedbergh, gives weight to this assumption. One other possibility is a connection with our old friend and guide, King Oswald of Northumbria. His constant companion was the raven and the local church dating back to Saxon times is called St Oswald's. It would be odd indeed if we had unwittingly been following in his footsteps since we left Hadrian's Wall at Heavenfield.

As well as the church, there are other antiquities that seem to indicate that Ravenstonedale had some especial quality as a centre of excellence. There is the ruin of a Gilbertine Priory, one of only twenty-six such houses in England, that lies next to the church. It has special significance as the Order was the sole monastic order to originate in Britain. Another is The Free Grammar School, founded by a Cambridge don in 1668, which was later the scene of a pupil rebellion. This, in itself, is not peculiar. In 1797 such was the general mayhem caused by the scholars of Rugby School that the militia had to be called in and the Riot Act read. The dispute at Ravenstonedale, however, has a more modern ring—a matter of pay and working conditions rather than the overthrow of despots. A conspiracy was hatched amongst the 'bigger boys' and after an assembly they rolled a large stone across the schoolroom door, thus barring the way of authority. After various demands for entry, a paper was passed through a window. This 'Bill of Rights' set out their case in rhyming couplets:

Of study we've plenty, of play scarce a bit
So hard is our study we are forced to submit

This continues at some length and the complaint concludes with a rather neat reversal against old adversaries who wish to ply them with the classics:

But Horace and Virgil and poets all say
That study's more pleasant united with play.

What follows is their offer. In return for studying hard, they would be given time to play. This included two days for Brough Fair, two days for 'nutting', a month at Christmas and the same at Midsummer, Sundays and Saints' Days for churchgoing and a day off to celebrate the monarch's birthday and the admission of a new scholar. They got all they asked for, with the exception of the Saints' Days, but one suspects that this was a makeweight they were prepared to sacrifice in a spirit of give and take. With no more ado and with the exception of a ceremonial 'rolling of the stone' on a yearly basis, the matter was quietly settled. ACAS would have been proud of the result.

All the above was to show that Ravenstonedale is more a particular than a peculiar place in the pejorative sense. Nevertheless, peculiar it is or, rather, Peculiar it was. The village was the seat of jurisdiction of the Peculiar of Ravenstonedale, an ecclesiastical court of twenty-four jurors selected from the local worthies. It had its own judicial powers and sets of regulations that it had the power to uphold. For the most part it was the usual stuff, the banning of football, prison sentences of up to ten months for bachelors who married outside the parish, and stiff fines if found playing cards or dice at any other time than during the twelve days before Christmas. That sort of thing. But there was one offence that might have been peculiar even to this Peculiar and that was the crime of eavesdropping or, as the parochial records had it, 'There shall neither man nor woman within this lordship lie or harken in any man's door or windows after the manner of an eaving dropper.' The fine for this heinous offence was 6s 8d.

Assuming you have threaded your way through this maze of potential litigation, you leave the village at Town Head, following a sign to Green Bell, and pull up onto the Howgills. Most people pass these hills on the way to higher things. Even Wainwright dismissed this offshoot of the Lake District as most suitable for those no longer able to climb anything worthwhile. But I feel this is a mistake. If you approach them from the north, as we are, they have an air of privacy much missing from the main Lakeland fells and are sufficiently compact that you can, on a single visit, make an intimate study of the area.

The choice of route is yours but will probably include the splendidly named Randygill Top, Kensgriff and Yarlside before the high point of The Calf is reached. Here you are standing at the very nub of the Yorkshire dales, five meandering glens, each emptying its river into the North Sea. Swale, Ure, Nidd, Wharfe, Aire. Sheffield United Never Win Away. It is curious what you can choose to recall from childhood memories. Thereafter, a long and easy ridge slopes down to Sedbergh, our next point of call. If you can arrange these matters, a fine summer's

evening is best suited to this descent, a perfect end to a satisfactory day. Some may think I am overstating the case and maybe I am. I have travelled up the M6 on hundreds of occasions over the last forty odd years but it is always where the road has to curve elegantly around the contours and jockey for position with the West Coast line that I feel pleasure has arrived and hassle left to settle in the dust.

Sedbergh has a Public Boarding School that specialises in breeding rugby players. It also has a Book Fair. The latter was born out of the Foot and Mouth epidemic of 2001 in an attempt to encourage visitors to the town. Much was made at the time of the losses incurred by farmers, with emotive pictures of funeral pyres lightening the evening skies, but the tourist trade suffered as much if not more when local commercial activity failed to be given its seasonal boost. As the then landlord of a famous Lakeland hotel put it, he would make less of a loss by buying and slaughtering every sheep in the district, if that meant the visitors could return. There is more to the relationship between walkers and the rural community than a code that ensures the former close gates and keep their dogs on a lead.

For my part, I was delighted to hear about the decision to make Sedbergh a centre for new and second-hand books. When I retired I received, among the usual plethora of Timepieces, Tankards and Thank You for Going Cards, a number of book tokens. With these I bought a current British Rail Passenger Timetable, the latest CAMRA *Good Beer Guide* and a copy of *Sheppard's Book Dealers in the British Isles*. They, along with the appropriate OS maps, were central to my Grand Retirement Plan. Thus armed, I would, at regular intervals, sally forth to places of interest and spend the time available poking around the local hostelries, hillsides and second-hand bookshops. Alas, the internet! The centrepiece of the day was the bookshop and from Cumbria to Worcestershire they were quickly disappearing. Times change. Recycling has now become a fad rather than a necessity and the easy access to information means that there are no longer any hidden gems. When it comes to books, even the charity shops know what they're at. What once was a shop where you could ferret around the shelves, counting on serendipity to throw up something of interest, is now a list on a television screen devoid of any character or appeal to the senses. So I, if not my bank manager, was delighted at Sedbergh's literary inspiration.

Leave the town, past the School, to Millthrop, where we join the Dales Way which leads over the western flanks of Long Rigg, past Gate Manor until, at Brakensgill Bridge, it meets the river Dee, which is more or less followed to reach the cobbled streets of Dent. More summer's evening stuff if possible. We are now approaching the next set of hills and County Tops appear, if not thick and fast, at least in close proximity. The first of these is Gragareth. It may be the highest point in Lancashire, as it now is, but it is far from the highest point around here. In fact, it is not even the highest point on its own separate ridge, being little more than a bump on the way up to Crag Hill. It was only when I was planning this route that I realised that I had visited this unprepossessing wart on two previous occasions. It is a stray, one that got over the wall. Never mind, it's quite a good place to look from, and another tick on our list.

Between Gragareth and Whernside, the highest point in North Yorkshire is Kingsdale, known locally as Little Switzerland. This sentimental affectation is commonly used to describe local beauty spots and a sweep through the web reveals such unlikely venues as Barbados and Hull. But the *nom de théâtre* given to the land between Kingsdale and its northern neighbour, Deepdale, is not based on some topographical quirk which might reveal a similarity to Kleine Scheidegg, but for the simple reason that it is often covered in snow and ice when other places in the locality are not. This can come as a surprise. At least it did to me when, one Christmas, I found myself in a car with an automatic gearbox sliding down a 1:5 slope of steep ice. It was not an unpleasant sensation, in fact one that people pay good money for at funfairs and the like, but the edge of my delight was somewhat blunted when I realised that at the foot of the hill the road turned sharp right through a narrow gateway. Failure to complete this manoeuvre meant a collision with a solid looking dry-stone wall. Nor did it help that on my right-hand side was a pretty steep drop and any application of the brakes might have upgraded the ride to Alton Towers proportions. Gravity pressed the accelerator and the automatic gearbox tumbled obediently through the ratios. Working on the assumption that if you are going to have a collision, choose something soft, I headed for the nearest snow-filled ditch. Little harm was done and several tractors later I was safely in Sedbergh, spending more than I meant on second-hand books.

No such fate should befall the humble pedestrian and by descending to the highest point on the road, you can pick up a path that runs up the western flank of Whernside. Before long you join the main drag, where it can seem as if you have emerged from a

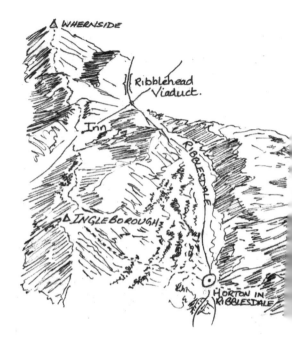

very minor slip road onto a motorway. For you are now on the circuit of the Three Peaks of Yorkshire and people are doing them, as the Three Peaks of Yorkshire—Whernside, Ingleborough and Pen-y-ghent—are what people do. The Army does them, Charity Walkers do them, Collectors of Badges to Stick on their Rucksacks do them. Some run, some walk, some even crawl, for the Three Peaks is no more or less than *A! Challenge! Walk!* In my experience, the

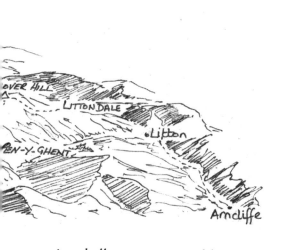

major challenge is to avoid being trampled to death in the rush. The route, the hills, the split times and records have been so sufficiently documented that there is little to add, other than that if you want to put your child off mountain walking for the rest of his or her life, an ascent of Whernside with its interminable false tops is as good a place as any to begin. Fortunately, we are descending to the Hill Inn before making the much more interesting ascent of

Ingleborough. Even this shapely hill has unpleasant memories. It was where I first saw the use of an off-road vehicle systematically destroying an ancient green lane. I write this immediately after reading in the local paper that such an anonymous vandal has partially destroyed the bridge at Three Shire Head, the alpha and omega of our expedition, which the Highway Authority is now obliged to repair at the expense of the ratepayer. It beggars belief that the general public, having paid a fee to the BBC which chooses to broadcast programmes that glamorise such anti-social activities, is then expected to pick up the tab for the damage. As for Pen-y-ghent, the Hill of the Winds, with its obviously Celtic name, appears a bit of an anomaly amongst a multitude of thwaites, sides and gills. Perhaps, at last, we have strayed beyond the recognised marches of Oz & Co.

As well as peaks, this area also boasts the Ribblehead Viaduct, which flickers in and out of the news as its relative stability threatens the existence of the much loved Settle–Carlisle line. In actuality, it is surprising it was built at all as much of the construction was completed in foul weather, with winds apparently gusting at 100mph. The tale is told that on one such occasion the wind was so strong one workman was blown over one side, under an arch, then back up onto his feet on the other. Well, we are in Yorkshire. Huddled nearby this edifice is the Station Inn, a feature of which is the Gentlemen's lavatory which has a transparent, as opposed to the normal frosted, glass window. The inscription reads 'Loo with a view'. The view being the viaduct and the bulk of Whernside. Unfortunately, on the only occasion I was able to contemplate this incomparable vista, the view was covered in thick mist. 'Bog in the fog' seemed more appropriate at the time.

From the top of Pen-y-ghent, you can either follow the Pennine Way north down a steep and, when wet, treacherous slope as far as Hull Pot, then, having peered into the gaping chasm, take a moorland path to Foxup. Alternatively, the ridge can be followed to Plover Hill, where an easier descent leads to the same destination. The river Skirfare is followed down Littondale to Arncliffe. This attractive village is worth a closer examination, if only to pause at the Falcon Inn. The inscription over the door sets the tone: Licensed only to sell ales, porter and tobacco. This is a rare restriction these days and is an indication of what is to come within. Stone flags, a series of serving hatches rather than a bar, and beer served straight from the barrel out of jugs, send the historical clock into reverse, to a time when inns offered succour to the weary rather than an alternative to cooking at home on a Sunday. The last step is due east over Old Cote Little Moor to Kettlewell, where we renew our acquaintanceship with the Dales Way.

— 6—
Writers, rats and reservoirs
Kettlewell to Flouch Inn

No more than a glance at the map shows that Kettlewell must be in an interesting position, for it is at the point where contours meet. The ridges that fall from over Old Cote Moor, Buckden Pike and Great Whernside form a nozzle through which the remnants of the Yorkshire Dales and Peaks are squeezed down Upper Wharfedale onto the commercial flood plain that has fostered the wealth of the county. Along with these waters flowed the real raw material, the men, women and children abandoning the uplands to fill the mills of Leeds and Bradford.

The Dales Way has taken a few bumpy rides before it arrives at this pleasant riverside meander. There is, however, one further lump to go. The path crosses Conistone Moor, taking a line high enough to offer good views into the surrounding dales and low enough to avoid the worst excesses of the limestone clints. Drystone walls are crossed by well designed stiles that have the arthritic in mind. It seems, however, that the more athletic sheep can also avail themselves of

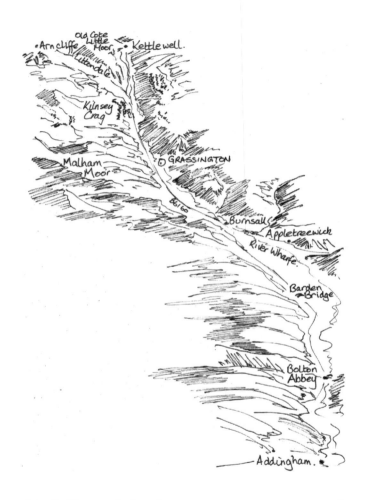

this facility as it has become necessary to top each stile with a heavily sprung gate. Once the natural limestone sculpture of Conistone Pie has been passed and Scot Gate Lane crossed, the Way drops pleasantly into Grassington and onto the water's edge.

Across the valley we get good views of Kilnsey Crag. In 1964 this imposing, top-heavy chunk of limestone was the location for a BBC documentary entitled *Operation Overhang*, featuring Pete Crew and Paul Nunn, who were among the leading climbers of the day. The *Radio Times*, heralding the cliff as 'where the Tigers sharpen their claws', described the problem as the 'dizziest and trickiest … most ferocious and sensational overhang in Britain', which was, on the night, compared to *walking on a ceiling!!!* It seems this hype did not completely capture the imagination of its intended audience and, after another attempt or two, most famously on The Old Man of Hoy, this particular bit of 'Grandstanding' fizzled out.

A few chunks of real estate in these parts were owned by the Dukes of Devonshire, who duly plundered the local minerals. Their success was followed by the usual Klondyke fever and such was the invasion of this peaceful dale that the police of Grassington were the first force in Britain to carry arms while on duty. But today there is no difficulty in following the route through Burnsall to Barden Bridge and the remains of Barden Tower, a once formidable fortification to repel any over-ambitious Scotsmen. It is, however, worth taking a very short diversion to the village of Appletreewick. For such a tiny place, it has a distinguished history. It appears in the Domesday Book and boasts two ancestral Halls and a spectral giant hound named the Barguest, an encounter with which means a sudden and violent death.

But its greatest glory is William Craven, who left his humble cottage in 1562 and in true Dick Whittington mode set off to London to make his fortune. By the time he was 21 he was a member of the Merchant Taylors' Guild and in the process of building a prosperous business; in 1611, he became Lord Mayor of London. With his newly acquired wealth he made an important contribution to the founding of St John's College, Oxford. More importantly for us, he lent his name to the village inn. The Craven Arms, a delightful little pub dating back to the sixteenth century, has a recently constructed Cruck Barn used for receptions and the like. The first such barn to be built in the district for over 300 years, it used the original method of construction. The crucks or 'A' frames were made from bent oak trees split down the middle to provide identical halves. These support the heather-covered roof and the outer shell. All the timbers are held together by wooden pegs, while traditional lime-and-horsehair plaster covers the walls. With its log fires and gas lighting, it must form an unusual and memorable atmosphere for its guests.

Between Barden and Bolton Bridges is the tourist honeypot of Bolton Abbey, where visitors are attracted by the natural and man-made splendours of the Strid Gorge and Bolton Priory. You may have to fight your way through the crowds, but you are now approaching Addingham and the end of the Way. After negotiating the hazards of the A59, the route again joins the river and, once past Low Park and High Mill, the town is reached. From Addingham to Ilkley, it first passes St Peter's Church, with its unusual blue-faced clock, then wriggles along lanes and superseded roads to Low Mill. We are now entering civilisation. There are moments when the humble rambler is allowed to walk along the river banks, but for the most part he or she is shepherded through the contrived corridors of social history to avoid any undue disturbance to members of the local golf and tennis clubs.

When I reached the end (or beginning) of the Dales Way, I realised that I was nearing the edge of a chasm spreading, even for the flying crow, for a considerable number of miles. I could get to the top of Ilkley Moor all right, but had little idea what happened on the other side. This grand canyon was not so much a hole in the ground as a hole in my knowledge and if, as intended, I avoided the Pennine Way, I had no idea of the lie of the land. The map was not obviously helpful. Among the clutter of small towns and villages, there were patches of greenery and wooded streams that suggested sinuous bypasses that might connect with a concertina of moorland and steep-sided valleys that lay further south. Then, once over the final hill at Manshead, there was an archipelago of reservoirs leading towards the Flouch Inn and home ground. The OS Explorer Series showed a plethora of green dots and, even more encouragingly, dashes, but memories of my previous experience amongst the collapsing stiles and barbed-wired gates between Pendle and Carnforth reminded me that a right of way could also lead to a rather uncomfortable rite of passage. The question was—how should I string it all together?

A closer examination showed that, in addition to the cartographical morse code, there were a good number of green lozenges. According to the map's key, these depicted various official Ways, of which, when it came to assembling the jigsaw, the Bradford Millennium, Calderdale and Kirklees appeared the most useful. If, as seemed probable, these local authorities had gone to some lengths to accommodate the interests of their constituents, it is likely that any barriers had been removed and broken stiles replaced. Throw in a couple of commercial publications like Mark Reid's *The Yorkshire Water Way* and Paul Hannon's *Trans-Pennine Way* and all started to fall into place. It seemed simply a matter of following the bouncing ball.

Readers of my previously expressed opinion on matters relating to waymarked routes may consider this to be a bit of a volte-face, but I would make a distinction between open countryside and urban sprawl. In the former, diligent use of the map and compass allows you to reach your desired destination with the minimum of fuss and without need for signposts. In the case of the latter, a mushrooming of slurry pits and housing estates can confuse the most careful of navigators and pitch them into some potentially awkward situations. As a result, it has always been my policy to avoid any of the local livestock, whether man or beast, that has a tendency to demonstrate an excess of proprietary zeal when you attempt to invade its territory. Gun-bearing yeomen, slavering rottweilers and posh girls on excitable horses tend to hold the higher ground when it comes to a debate on the right to roam.

Of the various Ways, the Millennium walk created by a group of Countryside Service volunteers is the most useful as it connects that moor where the absence of suitable headgear can lead to an untimely end involving worms and ducks and the spawning ground for the wild-eyed imagination of the Brontë girls. But before leaving Ilkley for Haworth you might consider some light refreshment. If you decide to rest awhile at one of the local hostelries, the Station Hotel is worth a visit, if only to admire the landlord's enterprise. No doubt fed up with visitors marching through the premises and availing themselves of his amenities without so much as a by-your-leave or buying a drink, he has erected within the bar a large arrowed sign marked TOILETS. This points towards a side entrance, with the implication that the facilities are situated in some outbuilding. On the wall in the passageway outside is another such sign. If you follow the instructions with care and, possibly by this stage, a little anxiety, you will find yourself once more outside the front door.

There is a variety of ways of reaching the moors above Ilkley, one of the most popular being via White Wells (once visited by optimistic invalids hoping to effect a cure for ailments ranging from arthritis to skin complaints by hurling themselves into baths of

ice-cold moorland water) and the various gritstone edges much used by rock climbers. All this area,

131

and the following stretch over Rombalds Moor to Weecher Reservoir, is an archaeologist's dreamland. The prehistoric cup and ring markings (first passed on Weetwood Moor), Bronze Age enclosures and the Lanshaw Lad who guided Anglo-Saxons across the moors, all still mark their place in history. Then there are the various Stones carved by man and nature. As to the significance or function of the Swastika Stone, Badger Stone or the Planets Rock we can only guess.

Once over the top of the moor, we descend, passing the Twelve Apostles and Horncliffe Well, a spring that has the reputation of never running dry, regardless of weather conditions, to reach Weecher Reservoir. After which a combination of lanes, tracks and footpaths take us past Golcar Farm to the edge of Baildon Moor and Shipley Glen. A visit to this wooded ravine was a popular excursion in Victorian times. Mill workers from the local towns and cities, no doubt happy to escape the grime and dust of their workplaces, arrived in great numbers. But where the tourist ventures, the entrepreneur is sure to follow. Local farmers added the sale of tea and scones to their commercial portfolio as visitors flocked to the 'Pleasure Grounds', with the renowned Aerial Glide (the first ever funfair ride) and the Japanese Gardens of Prod Lane.

It was a steep pull up from the valley to the glen and in 1895 Sam Wood built a cable-hauled funicular railway to assist the pleasure seekers to the top. Ever with an eye for making the extra penny, it also doubled as the Toboggan Run, where customers were hauled to the top, then, at top speed, hurtled on sledges down to the bottom. Unfortunately, in 1900, injuries occurred when one of the cars lost its coupling and the prototype Big Dipper had to be closed. An application of Health and Safety regulations that probably bewildered those children whose weekday job was to crawl around the innards of moving machinery in search of waste cloth. The tramway, however, supported by volunteers, still operates on a part-time basis.

Crossing the fifth of the great Yorkshire rivers and, once more, the Leeds–Liverpool Canal (last seen at Burnley), we enter Saltaire, a name that combines the river and the town's founder, Titus Salt. Salt, having made his money out of reducing alpaca into worsted cloth, turned philanthropist and, knowing full well the dreadful conditions that textile workers had to endure, set about building a mill town far from the pollution of Bradford. The mill, with the latest in smoke control technology, acted as the hub for the village. The town was built on a grid system, its streets each named after the owner's sense of allegiance to the Crown or, in an act of ultimate paternalism, his wife and eleven children. Every house was equipped with the utilities of running water and gas and abutted by its personal outside lavatory. In addition, recognising the traditional lifestyle of his workforce, he provided allotments for fresh produce and parkland for recreational activity. But this benevolence was not a one-way street. Salt understood not only that happy workers were good workers but also that he could now, as part of the deal, lay down certain ground rules. There were to be no trade unions or public houses, and the playing of football was strictly forbidden. But life moves on. On my first visit, I crossed the Aire to visit a bar in Victoria Road named Don't Tell Titus. It was a Saturday and the television was intoning the afternoon's football results: Coventry City 2 Sheffield United 0. Ah well, at least some things never change.

The way out of Saltaire is west along the Leeds–Liverpool before crossing it, the railway and the bypass into Beckfoot Lane which, in turn, crosses Harden Beck by a packhorse bridge at Beckfoot itself. Re-cross the beck and a golf course into Cottingley Wood. The next objective is Stephen Smith's Garden Centre, which can be reached by the rather convoluted wanderings of the Millennium Way, leapfrogging stiles and jumping over streams. The less energetic can reach the same objective along perfectly good tracks and past a rather well positioned folly. More woodland and a waterfalled stream lead to Hallas Bridge, where we part company from the Millennium project and make our own way to Oxenhope. Our route passes south of Cullingworth, along Hallas Lane, crosses the Hewenden Road and a dismantled railway to reach the busy A629 at a series of disused quarries much loved by the exponents of scrambling around on motorbikes. A right of way skirts this general exuberance and leads over Black Moor before dropping to the station at Oxenhope.

During the walk from there to Pecket Well, I was accompanied by a friend who had just returned from a holiday in the Swiss Alps. On the way to Leeshaw Reservoir he waxed lyrical on flower-bedecked alpine meadows and glaciers glistening in the evening sunlight. Once we had reached the lane that leads to Stair and the edge of the wilder country around Bodkin Top, I detected a note of deeper introspection. Although far too polite to mention it, it was clear that my companion was engrossed in a private debate between the relative merits of his recent vacation and his current outing. Not, I imagined, to the advantage of the surrounding environment.

The day was in one of those moods where, too sullen to rain, it pervaded the air with an embracing dampness and covered the hawthorn in a film of drip. The ground was generally muddy and where man and beast had crowded together to negotiate some constriction between gorse and rock, it was a quagmire. As we gained height, the draught increased, encouraging the damp to share our bodily warmth by seeking comfort within the seams of our outer clothing. My companion lapsed into silence. Clearly, night had fallen on the Jungfraujoch.

Yet I was pleased, for this is how it should be. To my right was Haworth Moor with its ruin at Top Withins, the supposed site of the windswept Wuthering Heights. Further west lies Stanbury Moor, which in 1824 was the scene of an exploding bog. No one is certain of the cause but on 2nd September at around six o'clock in the evening there was an almighty explosion following a sudden storm. Two chasms were cleft in the moor, the larger being twelve feet deep and 700 yards across, and tons of earth and stone were swept down the hillside on a torrent of water. On the moors at the time were the Brontë children who, as they fled for shelter, could scarcely have guessed that they, in turn, would cause an even greater explosion on the English literary scene.

Although Charlotte had a perceptive eye for her surroundings—'a scene of wet lawn and storm-beat shrub with ceaseless rain sweeping away wildly' *(Jane Eyre)*, 'The skies hang full and dark, a wrack from the west; the clouds cast themselves into strange forms' *(Villette)*, and Anne chipped in with 'the soil was thin and poor; bits of grey rock here and there peeped out from the grassy hillocks; bilberry-plants and heather, relics of a more savage wilderness, grew under the wall' *(The Tenant of Wildfell Hall)*—it is Emily, in her only novel, who shows the more intimate sense of place. Those who tread the southern Pennine moors, and especially the solitary walker who prefers not people but the unbeaten track, will quickly recognise what she is about. They will, without difficulty, connect the image with the actuality of the narrative and see how the land, soggy and infertile, with a uniformity that makes navigation difficult, pervades the mood of the story, that death by drowning is a metaphorical as well as a real possibility, and that Catherine and the moors are one.

The vicarage at Haworth, the family home of the Brontës, is a must-tick visit for the literary pilgrim. Sadly, this industry, with its sentimental approach, has done much to belittle the literary worth of Emily's novel, a state compounded by the original cinematic adaptation, with Laurence Olivier and Merle Oberon, that cut chunks of the narrative and diminished the plot to the level of a Mills & Boon. Such a treatment does not tell even the half of it. The novel is as much about revenge, class envy and the strengths and weakness of a society cut off from the main streams of civilisation as it is about love. As Martin Kettle, columnist for *The Guardian*, pointed out, 'If *Wuthering Heights* is a love story, then *Hamlet* is a sitcom.'

The narrative, for the most part, is told by a servant Nelly Dean, but with such assurance that it immediately alerts its readers to the possibility that they are hearing a partial version of the tale. The essence of this story of unreconciled relationships lies in its ambiguity. Why did Earnshaw bring a stray child back from his visit to Liverpool? Might Heathcliff have been his illegitimate child? Would this explain Catherine's confused reaction to the possibility of marriage? It has been argued it was the Brontës who first forced the world of Romantic thought and poetry into the framework of the novel and ended an age of polite fiction penned by and for refined young ladies. This may not be entirely fair, but one thing's for sure: those readers who wish to discover the secrets of the wild country would be better advised to read

Wuthering Heights than accompany Miss Austen on her jaunt up the wooded slopes of Box Hill.

Once the summit has been passed, you quickly fall into the shelter of Crimsworth Dean and drop down through the woods to Midgehole. Immediately climb up the steep valley side, a feature you will experience more than once during the next few miles, to reach Pecket Well. You are now on the Calderdale Way, which contours around the perimeter of Midgley Moor with extensive views into the valley and across to Stoodley Pike. After Cock Hill you reach a standing stone known locally as Churn Milk Joan and there is a tradition of placing a coin in the hollow on its top for good luck. Its name and tradition may derive from the milk churns that were left for collection by local villagers who placed money as payment in the 'honesty box' on the stone's apex.

This rough obelisk stands on Crow Hill and gives its name to a poem written by the former Poet Laureate, Ted Hughes, and below us lies the town of Mytholmroyd, his birthplace. At one stage in *Wuthering Heights*, Lockwood interrupts the narrative recounted by Nelly Dean, commenting rather patronisingly that, despite her lowly station, the servant had a fine understanding of matters —no doubt as she had been 'compelled to cultivate

[her] reflective faculties for want of occasions for frittering [her] life away in silly trifles'. Maybe there is something in the local air, for there is no doubt that Hughes took the opportunity to 'cultivate' his reflective faculties when it came to describing the surroundings of his formative years. He was a man, as they say, who noticed things and his work reflects the keenness of his observation. Anyone who can craft lines about the local landscape like 'Even its grimace is empty, / Warted with quartz pebbles from the sea's womb.' (Still Life) or 'Here is the fern's frond, unfurling a gesture, / Like a conductor' (Fern) must have his eyes and wits about him.

The above quotes are from a collection entitled *Wodwo* that includes poetry, drama and prose. If you have an ambition to understand what the poet is about, this is as good a place as any to start. As Hughes implies in his introductory Author's Note, the stories can throw light on the poems and the circumstances from which they were wrought. Whilst writers of the Brontës' era could cull tragedy from the deprivation caused by poverty, ill health and social inequality, a writer in the second half of the twentieth century lived in an age where social advances had sufficiently blunted these obvious agents of destruction. Hughes had to write about new battles now that old foes

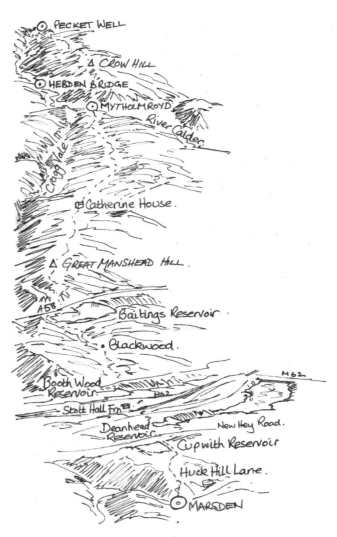

⊙ PECKET WELL

△ CROW HILL

⊙ HEBDEN BRIDGE

⊙ MYTHOLMROYD

River Calder

Cragg Vale

⊠ Catherine House.

△ GREAT MANSHEAD HILL.

A58

Baitings Reservoir.

• Blackwood.

Booth Wood Reservoir.

M62

M62

Stott Hall Frm ⊞

Deanhead Reservoir.

New Hey Road.

Cupwith Reservoir

Huck Hill Lane.

⊙ MARSDEN

had been vanquished, and peer more deeply into the turmoil that lies between sentimental expectation and the reality of the actual. A repeated approach in his prose is to observe human frailty through the prism of animal behaviour.

When animals appear in *Wuthering Heights*, they are seen as subservient to their human owners. Dogs are there to defend their master's property, horses to act as a form of transport. When they appear in Hughes' stories, they take a more central role to comment on the human condition. In 'The Harvesting', Mr Grooby, a man apparently of some substance, has the shooting rights at a local farm. The farmer is harvesting the crop in ever-decreasing circles, driving the rabbits from their cover for the shooter to kill. Grooby, although convalescing from some debilitating illness, stubbornly stays out in the blazing sun, convinced there is still more quarry to shoot. Twice the tension builds as the rectangle of wheat gets smaller, the temperature rises, the farmer gesticulates, the stookers' dogs strain at the leash. Twice a hare emerges, Grooby fires and faints, then fires and faints, again the 'cutter blade blurred into life' before, at last, a single terrible scream like a child in agony. In those confused and repeated moments, the hunter and hunted become one.

It is this interaction between man and animals that often seems to drive Hughes' work. The animals are mostly those we fear or, at least, are suspicious of—foxes, crows wolves, all embodied in the mythical goblin-like monster of the Wodwo that is the collection's title. In 'Sunday', it is rats. On this particular Sabbath, Billy Red is making an appearance at the Top Wharf pub to demonstrate, in return for free drinks, his prowess of killing rats with his bared teeth. What the audience have come to see is the previously ensnared rodents, one by one, being allowed to escape and, as they do, Billy pouncing, catching them by the neck and worrying them to death. Amongst the observers is the narrator, a young boy previously excited by the prospect, but who quickly leaves after the first death. Another, a young woman, brought along by her boyfriend, slips out as soon as she realises the implications of what is going to happen. The two meet on the towpath in mutual, unspoken condolence. Meanwhile, inside the pub, the men, fuelled by beer, applaud their own vicarious sense of dominance.

The most significant of these stories, at least from our point of view, is entitled 'The Rain Horse'. The protagonist has returned to his home town and is making a nostalgic tour of his childhood haunts in the surrounding countryside. It starts to rain and he is taking shelter in a wood when a horse that he has previously seen on the skyline 'running on its toes like a cat, like a dog up to no good' came thundering through the trees as if to run him down. Bewildered by the animal's apparently irrational behaviour, he tries to find a way back to the safety of human habitation. But the horse seems to second-guess his every move and cuts off each chosen line of retreat. Now convinced that the animal is 'definitely after him', he decides to stand his ground and fight. The horse duly charges and the man starts to hurl rocks which eventually stops the animal in its tracks. The experience seems to be over and he heads back up the hill, his new suit ruined by the rain and ankle-deep mud. As the pulse rate slackens, he feels 'as if some important part had been cut out of his head'.

Although I first read this story some decades ago, I felt an immediate sense of recognition as, on a pleasant summer's evening, I started to descend from the summit of Crow Hill. Surely this was the very place where the story was set. That must be the wood that was little more than a quarry and that the rectangle of scrub oak separated by an empty field. It was also not difficult to imagine Mytholmroyd, squatting in the valley below, as 'the blue shoal of the town ... rising and falling ... in the pale, swaying backdrop of rain'. Of course, Hughes might have set the story in any of a dozen similar places but I still kept a wary eye open. No need really. Rain Horses don't appear when the sun shines.

The way from Mytholmroyd to the top of the moor is the inevitable hard work, but at least Stake Lane had been built with horse and cart in mind, rather than ascensionists of the North Face of the Eiger. Would-be Tour de Franceurs could limber up on the climb through Cragg Vale, the longest continuous road gradient in the country, to reach the A58 which runs parallel to and at the same height as the M62. I had taken the Stake Lane option as it would connect with Miry Lane and Coppy Nook Lane, which both pointed in the right direction. As I ascended, I began to tot up the number of lanes I had walked along since I left Ilkley Moor. Quite a lot. Some you could drive along, some had degenerated into rough and twisting tracks, whilst others had become so overgrown that they were little more than paths. So what is a lane? The word is Old English in origin and means a passageway between hedges, banks or similar, a permitted route through an organised agrarian structure. Which was the chicken and which the egg? Did they plan fields around the existing thoroughfares or was the pedestrian, as now, forced to pick his way amongst the Anglo-Saxon property developers and similar chancers? Our lanes eventually peter out in the moorland of Great Manshead Hill, traversed, courtesy of Yorkshire Water, by a permissive path (perhaps though, in these days of open access, it tends to the promiscuous) and from its highest point, we can at last see the Peak District once more. Below is Baitings Reservoir, the first link in the waterland chain that we will now begin to follow.

From Baitings to Flouch Inn is a complex piece of land, and route-finding along a series of footpaths, bridleways, Water Board access lanes and disused railways can be quite tricky. En route, it wends through reservoirs, tunnels under the M62 and negotiates the human infiltration of West Yorkshire. To untie these knots, I wholeheartedly recommend the route suggested by Mark Reid in *The Yorkshire Water Way,* Volume 2, to provide, at least, a framework for your journey. The only reservation being that over-reliance on the immutability of pedestrian thoroughfares can produce unexpected difficulties. While crossing this section of land at precisely the moment when I was as far from any transport support as possible, I came across a notice announcing the temporary closure of a footpath across the isthmus that separated two rather large reservoirs. Closer inspection revealed that there was no way of ignoring the order as the whole area had been fenced off, patrolled by guard dogs and, probably, men with machine guns. As, like Macbeth, returning were as tedious etc, I was forced to add a not-inconsiderable detour to a journey rapidly approaching dusk.

This is not all as grim as it sounds. One of the advantages of the latest laying-waste of the North is that old eyesores have been allowed to succumb to nature and we meet ivy-clad ruins that have all the appearance of ruined Inca temples in a Peruvian jungle. Even the man-made intrusion of reservoirs (fourteen are passed in the twenty-five miles being described) has merged into the surroundings, with the scars of building now virtually healed. Moreover, the combination of hillside and water is always pleasing to the eye and, as man-made constructions go, reservoirs can in certain lights have a charm of their own. Their existence, at least, supports the health and well-being of the community, which is more than can be said for masts that enable the transmission of twitter or even the supply of electricity to activate dish-washing machines.

I was pulling up from Deanhead Reservoir to the New Hey Road when I began to comprehend the full

implications of my chosen route. If I continued to follow the mark of Reid, I would be forced back into Marsden and would have to retrace my northbound journey to Wessenden Head. This meant that my original plan of a Great North Circular would become more of a Loop the Loop, and as the strangulation of urban sprawl was beginning to bite, the whole project seemed to be about to hit the buffers. (Whilst this metaphorical amalgam will certainly excite disapprobation in literary circles, it is an accurate representation of my general confusion at the time.)

The better plan might have been to leave the Pennine Way during my northern leg at Black Hill and, striking across Featherbed Moss, to intercept the Station to Station Walk from Marsden to Littleborough at a suitable juncture. There again, it would still be possible to avoid Marsden for the second time by swinging east at Cupwith Reservoir and sticking together bits of the Calder Way, reach Shooters Nab and eventually cross Meltham Moor to join Nether Lane on the Kirklees Way.

As I plodded on, this general confusion appeared to resolve itself in the form of a patter song so beloved by the Victorian Music Hall.

From Baitings to Booth Wood is fairly straightforward
Y'd scarcely get lost by the Head of the Dean,
But Cupwith to Digley gets all higgly-piggly
If you want to avoid where once you have been.

Taking Butterley, Blakely, the Wessenden double
Is a sensible choice but you've been there before.
And all other options are little but trouble
When you catch it on Cop Hill, then more upon Moor.

Dodging shooters and hooters and hoodies on scooters
Will allow you to cross to the Hill of the Deer…
Yet hold not a fear—be it ever so wiggly—
Each road that you choose will land you at Digley.

The rest of the way is virtually downhill
First Holme (if not dry) ere Winscar is met
After wending your way twixt Ramsden & Brownhill
You'll be seeing the end of a very Langsett.

I expect Sir William Schwenck Gilbert would have made a rather better fist of it.

In the end, it turned out easy enough to join the connecting blobs of terra firma in a reasonably coherent way. Moreover, there are, at least, two points of interest. The first is the dam at Booth Wood Reservoir which holds back a bulge of water over a mile long and around 200 yards wide at its broadest point. As you pass beneath its impressive span, realisation dawns about the implications of the raids of 617 Squadron on the Möhne and Eder dams. The other is Stott Hall Farm which stands, apparently recalcitrant, in the middle of the east and westbound carriageways of the M62. Urban legend has it that the farmer resolutely refused to sell and it stands as a monument to the triumph of the individual over faceless bureaucracy but, in fact, the danger of landslip dictated the eventual location of the carriageways. Nevertheless, seeing it for the first time on a typical Pennine day, with the mist spilling off Saddleworth Moor and your view distorted by the backlash of speeding lorries, you could be forgiven for thinking it some spectral Marie Celeste, shaking its fist at the inexorable abrasion of progress.

Finally, after departing the last of the reservoirs at Winscar and following a disused railway line that bursts out of the hillside into the village of Dunford Bridge, we realise that, at last, this leg of the journey is coming to an end. A fact confirmed when the welcoming sight of the Flouch Inn looms into view.

—7—

In our beginnings are our ends
Flouch Inn to home

If you've stopped going up, it must be Howden Edge and you have reached the most remote point on the Derwent Watershed Walk. This forty-mile challenge encapsulates the nature of the Dark Peak, crossing as it does both Kinder and Bleaklow, as well as the easier going of Win Hill and Mam Tor. It was first completed by a party led by the legendary Eustace Thomas who, among other feats, completed seventy-nine miles and 30,000 feet of Lake District fells in little over twenty-eight hours. For those interested in undertaking such expeditions, there is an excellent illustrated account in *The Big Walks*, compiled by Ken Wilson and Richard Gilbert.

You have managed this collision with no man's land by climbing from the Flouch Inn via Cut Gate, one of the oldest rights of way in the Peak. To the south and a little east lies Margery Hill, unlucky thirteen—at least for me, who has never seen the summit without rain. So, not surprisingly, given the charm of its isolation, this area was the scene of a second mass trespass, which took place five months after the invasion of

Kinder. Unlike the Manchester Ramblers' Federation, who condemned the demonstration, the Sheffield Ramblers' Federation was more pro-active. Although it would not officially commit its own organisation to support the venture, it encouraged individual clubs who backed the motion to join together and organise the protest. This was a more violent affair than the earlier confrontation, and at Abbey Brook a hundred or more gamekeepers armed with cudgels set about the ramblers. The police, already chary as a result of the trial of the Kinder ringleaders, and having every reason to believe that the track in question was a legal right of way, kept a low profile and refused the keepers' demands that arrests should be made, instead urging them to minimise the physical damage they were inflicting.

As with the Kinder Trespass, the Establishment suspected other and more sinister motives. Among the clubs that took part were the Brightside Independent Labour Party, Spartacus, which had been set up by the Sheffield Young Communist League, and the Independent Labour Party Guild of Youth, and it would have appeared to the conspiracy theorists that their presence was more moved by political ambition than a desire for exercise and fresh air. But it was not all would-be revolutionaries. The Onward Rambling

Club also sent representatives and if their handbook for the season 1929–30 is anything to go by, they were not a particularly aggressive lot. In addition to the usual details of times and locations for the various gatherings, there was a stern note of introduction on how members should conduct themselves when rambling in the countryside. There was also an injunction to Meet Leaders that, as well as keeping a wary eye open for any careless decanting of orange peel, they should 'see to it that a song is sung during the day, for to sing is to be happy'.

Amongst the obligatory and not so deathless prosody, there were various articles relating to rambling matters. In one extract, from 'Going about the Country with your Eyes Open' by Owen Jones and Marcus Woodward, there is an explanation of the Law of Access as it then stood. This included the established precedent that if a gamekeeper suspected that a walker, even if on a right of way, was attempting to drive game or otherwise interfere with a shoot, he, or others in authority, were legally entitled to sit on the offender until the danger had passed. Listed among the illegal *modus operandi* were the over-doffing of hats as if in greeting and the ostentatious flourishing of handkerchieves when in the act of blowing the nose. There was also an article

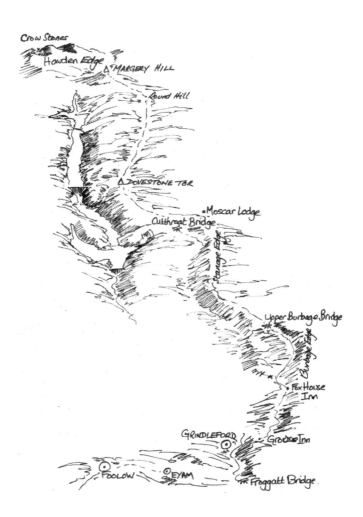

Crow Stones

Howden Edge

△ MARGERY HILL

Round Hill

△ DOVESTONE TOR

• Moscar Lodge

Cutthroat Bridge

Stanage Edge

Upper Burbage Bridge

Burbage Edge

• Fox House Inn

GRINDLEFORD

• Grouse Inn

• FOOLOW

• EYAM

Froggatt Bridge

by the Chief Scout, Lord Robert Baden-Powell, who described the value of climbing as one that gets 'you to face the difficulties of life in the same spirit'. This extract came from *Rovering to Success*, a publication heartily recommended by the editor as one that would help young men 'past the obstacles of: Horses, Wine, Women, Cuckoos and Irreligion'. Perhaps I have been too hard on the landowners, beset as they were, on one hand by anarchists bent on bestial horrors and poisoning wells, and on the other by troupes of hanky-waving hikers singing interminable choruses of 'Gin, Gan, Gooli, Gooli, Watcha'.

After leaving Margery Hill, we continue to follow the Watershed Walk to reach our next objective, Stanage Edge. Curiously enough, we are once more in Brontë country, for it was when Charlotte was staying at the vicarage in Hathersage that she discovered the surname Eyre on nearby tombstones, and it is quite possible that Thornfield Hall was inspired by the graceful splendour of New Lees Hall. But the moors in these parts seem less desolate than those surrounding Haworth, for the gritstone escarpments that can at times appear grim and foreboding, now face south and west and are often softened by sunlight.

There are two ways to reach the Edge and either way we have to cross the Snake Road, so called not because of its winding nature but after the Snake Inn, which had as its emblem the serpent that featured in the Cavendish Arms of the Duke of Devonshire. The first of these crossings is at Cutthroat Bridge, where four centuries ago a man was found with his gullet slit. He was still alive when discovered but, despite the best efforts of his rescuers, died not long after. There was no such hiatus in a recent and more bizarre case where Anthony Antoniou decapitated his step-father with a Japanese ceremonial sword and dumped the body at the same location. A less violent alternative is to cross the A57 at Moscar Lodge, which has the advantage of landing you at the very start of the Stanage outcrop. 'Outcrop', however, is a rather inadequate description. The rocks extend for around three miles, allowing the possibility of hundreds of separate climbs at all standards.

Of all the Edges, Stanage is the best known to the climbing fraternity and has always attracted the top climbers of their day. From the early pioneering efforts of J W Puttrell, the 'last great problems' have been sought out and solved. The names of these code-crackers, F C Aldous, H M Kelly, A S Piggott, Colin Kirkus, Maurice Linnell and, most famously, Joe Brown and Don Whillans, read like a Roll of Honour and by the 1960s they and their supporting casts had discovered and completed nearly five hundred separate climbs. Since then, the elimination has continued, producing many notable routes, among which The Archangel by Ed Drummond and Jerry Moffat's Ulysses are milestones.

Amid the spear-carriers, one individual stood out, not so much for his climbing as his presence. Rice Kemper Evans, American Vice-Consul in Sheffield, who reigned over Stanage during the early Twenties, was a larger-than-life character, introducing visiting experts to his favourite climbs in a proprietorial manner and bribing the gamekeepers with barrels of beer. He suddenly disappeared, leaving the climbing world not, as he had hoped, with a host of noteworthy climbs but with the term 'layback', which he allegedly coined to describe this tricky off-balance move.

The line of rocks continues over Burbage, Froggatt, Curbar and Baslow Edges before finally petering out at Birchen's and the welcome sight of the Robin Hood Inn. Although we are going to leave at Froggatt, there is a classic walk, again documented by Wilson and Gilbert, which runs from the Flouch Inn to the Robin Hood, a distance of some twenty-five miles. This is a decent enough outing in itself, but if you are an exponent of bog-trotting and climbing, you might consider the following challenge conceived by two

Birmingham mountaineering clubs, the Ceunant and the Cave & Crag. The course is roughly the section between Stanage End and the Robin Hood, but with a few detours to include every major gritstone crag in the locality. The event has a competitive element and the rules to decide the 'winner' are as follows. A rope of two chooses its intended grade and climbs one route on each of the fourteen crags (Stanage is split into three areas) within a stated time. Points are awarded as follows: 2 points for each climb at the intended grade, -1 point for the grade below, +1 for the grade above, 1 point for each star (as defined in agreed guidebooks) and a bonus of 1 point for every route over nine completed. The Worcester Mountain-eering Club runs a similar event, sometimes known as the Gritstone Gallop, where competitors have to complete the journey on foot. Or, as one participant put it: 'The idea is to hurtle from crag to crag, notch-ing up as many stars as possible, barely pausing to stuff down a sandwich and speeding off again. Insane? Of course. But isn't that why we do it?'

But all this activity inevitably had its drawbacks. Even in the 1930s, thousands of tourists, climbers and walkers would flood the area at weekends. Most of them, however, travelled by public transport, train, bus or tram. They arrived at Grindleford, Hathersage or the Fox House Inn, then dispersed on foot, each group at its own pace. Now ninety-five percent come by car and, as half the population of England lives within sixty miles of Stanage, in far greater numbers. They began to clog up the narrow lanes and fill every available parking space. This caused them to tread the same tracks, polish the same climbs, litter the same spots. Clearly some control had become necessary. In 1996, Pay and Display machines appeared in the Stanage car parks and the estate introduced earth mounding to prevent roadside parking. Uproar followed. Having thrown off the yoke of private ownership, it now seemed that access was being strangled by the tentacles of bureaucracy. The BMC mounted a campaign and stickers demanding free access appeared in car windows. In truth, it was more diplomatic incompetence than Stalinist pogrom. The authorities agreed that they should have consulted more widely and eventually the dust settled.

Nevertheless, something needed and still needs to be done. The solution seems simple. First, provide, within the Park, an efficiently run system of public transport with appropriate facilities for rucksacks, pushchairs and the like. The provision should fit the need, from eco-friendly trains to 'Mountain Goat' stop-on-request buses to reach less accessible areas.

Runabout tickets to cover all eventualities should be readily available at a minimal cost. If the carrot does not work and the general public does not value how much it is saving in petrol and frayed nerves, then the stick of a Park, Pay and Ride should become obligatory for all visitors. Above all, the emphasis should be on what the majority of the public wants, rather than what turns a penny. Perhaps then we might remember that recreation is meant to be a change from, not an extension of, the daily grind.

We only follow the grit as far as Froggatt, where we turn south past the Chequers Inn to cross the river Derwent at Froggatt Bridge. Finally, after clipping the edge of Stoke Wood, we reach a track which leads to what appears to be a private graveyard. Closer inspection shows that it is the final resting place of a family who died of the Plague. Such deaths, at the time, were not uncommon but what was uncommon at that or any other time were the circumstances. For we are now approaching the Plague Village, Eyam. In late August 1665, George Vicars, the village tailor, was no doubt pleased to receive the bundle of cloth he had ordered from London. What he had no way of realising was that there were additional passengers in the parcel. When he spread it out to dry in front of the fire, the heat activated the fleas buried between the folds. These fleas, parasites of the black rat, were plague carriers.

On 7th September, Vicars died of a violent fever and it was clear the illness was likely to spread through the whole area and that a number of villagers must already be infected. Although some fled, the majority were persuaded by their rector, William Mompesson, to stay in the village and thus limit the contagion. Outsiders left food and other necessaries at the boundary stones and were in turn paid in coins that had been left in scooped stones filled with vinegar. Throughout the next twelve months death swept through the community, but by 1st November 1666 the last of its victims had died and the danger had passed.

Although, like most people, I was moved by the selfless nature of the action, I was also struck by the way it contrasted with the behaviour of that other village group whose history I had earlier crossed. Whereas, at Pendle, the Christian faith had invoked vindictiveness and a sanctimonious sense of moral superiority, the same belief had persuaded a similar community, despite fear of imminent death, to put others first. Out of a population of 350, 260 died, yet their decision probably saved the lives of thousands in the North of England. As you would expect, stories of self-sacrifice and loss abound. Perhaps one of the most affecting was the courtship of Emmott Sydall and Rowland Torre from a neighbouring village. They met on opposite sides of the hollow of Cucklett Delf, uttering their protestations across the rocky gulf, until the day when Emmott failed to appear. Star-cross'd lovers separated by a barrier that puts into perspective the petty squabbling of Montagues and Capulets.

Out of this tragedy an unlikely benefit may have emerged. Despite being in daily contact with the contamination, first nursing, then burying her husband and six children, Elizabeth Hancock survived, and there were other similarly placed individuals who were entirely unaffected. No doubt the rector had an explanation based on individual goodness but it is unlikely to have included the possibility of a genetic flaw. Recent research into the disease of Aids has shown that certain individuals can contract the virus, yet prevent it from interfering with their immune system. This has been put down to the presence of a mutated gene known as Delta 32. Scientists then wondered whether this could happen with other such viruses, of which the bubonic plague was one. The isolated village of Eyam was seen as an ideal opportunity to test the theory. After much historical research, the individual survivors were identified and descendants

traced. Checking the DNA of these, it was found that a significant percentage had the selfsame genetic mutation. Perhaps, in years to come, a remarkable decision made in a remote community will be more far-reaching than anyone ever imagined.

Once we have left Eyam, the route is effectively along footpaths to Foolow, where a neat side-step around the duck pond enables us to reach Wardlow Mires and cross the A623 into Cressbrook Dale. We are now in limestone country and one of the delights

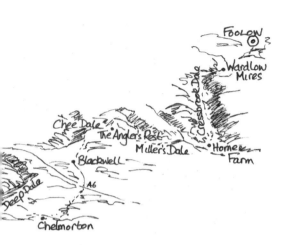

of the Peak is its softer cream centre encompassed in the dark chocolate of the gritstone horseshoe. The deep, heavily vegetated valleys with glints of gleaming white rock hidden beneath the foliage stand in stark contrast to the moorland we have crossed since leaving Ilkley, giving a signal that the North is coming to an end. We are now in the land of Izaac Walton and the Lazy Trout. John Constable could well be just around the corner. We join the river Wye and Miller's Dale at Home Farm and, after passing directly under (avoid the bouncing climber) the crag of Water-cum-Jolly, a sort of outdoor, indoor climbing wall, the river is crossed at Litton Mill, where the path climbs to join a disused railway line, now the Monsal Trail.

We can continue on this high-level route until the river comes up to join us, then, a little before Chee Tor, swing south to Blackwell Hall. Alternatively, just before the railway crosses the road, we can drop back both into the valley and, given appropriate timimg, the Angler's Rest for lunch. This is another gem on the circuit, providing excellent food and an interesting variety of cask ales. It also has a separate room for bemuddied walkers. A visit is well worth the pull back up the hill to the abandoned Miller's Dale station, sadly now the obligatory car park. Whichever the way, after Blackwell we cross the A6 and disappear through the back of a wardrobe into our next port of call.

To say that Chelmorton is a medieval village is a clear exaggeration—buses have been known to arrive from Buxton. But, like Ravenstonedale, it lies in its own traffic-free triangle, so it's not a place you go through accidentally. Though, if you should, you would get the sense of another age. The church, the highest in Derbyshire, is of Norman origin and the street plan is thought to have been little altered since Saxon times. Most significant is the prochronistic field pattern, still laid out in the common medieval practice of strips. The Church Inn, formerly the Blacksmith's Arms, is of a later foundation but was nevertheless enlarged from a building as old as the church and stands within suitable repenting distance of it.

From Chelmorton we aim for Buxton Country Park, crossing the heads of Deep and Cow Dale. It is a good idea to enter the Park at Poole's Cavern, and an even better one to visit this series of limestone chambers. Though named after a fifteenth-century outlaw who used them as a hideaway, there is evidence that they have from earliest times been the site of human habitation. As a tourist attraction, the Cavern has long been admired and in the sixteenth century was proclaimed 'The first Wonder of the Peak'. Of particular interest are the stalactites, including one known, with some justification, as 'the flitch of bacon'.

We are now at the final moments of the journey and leave the Country Park, passing Grinlow Tower, better known locally as Solomon's Temple. Built on a Bronze Age barrow by the local landowner to relieve the unemployed, it offers a particularly fine view from its upper parapets. After skirting the Terret plantation we join the A54 (A537). This stretch of tarmac from Buxton to Macclesfield, much beloved by motorcyclists attempting to hold the perfect racing line, is regularly described as the most dangerous in Britain. It may well be, but it is also the most scenic. Perhaps it's best seen in early spring when, after passing the Cat and Fiddle (a possible diversion for a final drink) the evening sun glints off frosted snow caught in stone-wall crevices and throws into relief the Cheshire Plain with its backdrop of Welsh hills.

It is around here that you cross the border into Staffordshire, a dubious contender for membership of the exclusive Counties of the North. However, this most northerly section of the rest of England does its best and, with a final grunt, drags the heather and bog sufficiently far south to justify inclusion—and would also remind you that Cheeks Hill, its highest point, is almost as far north as Cheshire's Shining Tor. As if to clinch matters, on my last visit it played host to a red kite which, with a flash of fork-tailed rust, slid out of view in pursuit of supper. Yet if I was disparaging about the mountainous merits of Gragareth, that lump's failure to impose is as nothing when compared with the efforts of Cheeks Hill. To reach this ultimate eminence, you have to cross over Axe Moor, which is higher than your objective but, significantly, still in Derbyshire. But I suppose Cheeks Hill has some claim to fame. It is the only summit I have ever conquered while going downhill.

As I left the summit of the final top and made my way down the stony track that leads to the packhorse bridge at Three Shire Head, I realised that the walk was over and began to wonder what, if anything, I had achieved. Or, to put it another way, apart from the obvious statistics of engineering a continuous route of 700 miles and a circuitous variety of ascents and descents between sea level and the highest point of England, what I had learnt about the true nature of the North.

Most striking is its Tardis-like structure. In one sense, it is small and compact. You are never far from a road and the start and finish of most of the separate stages can be reached by public transport. In another, when you keep to the high ground, there is often a sense of endless expanse and, when the weather turns in on you, of desolate loneliness. Two further things stuck out. The first was the proliferation of rights of way that had been established over centuries and have now been thoroughly signposted, documented and brought to heel by the individual local authorities. The second, that, apart from the Lakeland fells and their outliers, much of the high-level walking had been over moorland and more moorland. These two observations are not unconnected. Nearly all such ground was good for very little and, by tradition, classified as waste. This lack of proprietorial concern meant that it was regarded by all parties as common land to be used as they thought fit, though mostly as a short cut between scattered settlements. Thus 'Ways', from time immemorial, had been established, first, to facilitate the conveyance of commerce or coffins, then, in due course, to suggest an opportunity for invigorating exercise and exploration.

Yet, in all this wilderness, one creature seemed able to flourish among the bog and heather. Unfortunately for the red grouse, its flight pattern offered a not over-difficult target for sportsmen who, given sufficient care and organisation, could slaughter their quarry in bragworthy numbers. One set of demands conflicted with the other and the ensuing struggle between landowners who could turn their shoots to profit and those who saw the land as ideal for healthy recreation was almost inevitable. Investigation of legal rights became duly rigorous. Associations like the Peak and Northern and the Ramblers used their expertise to represent the interests of the walker at tribunals and arbitration. Landowners, in turn, leant on the arbitrators. What at one time might have been a matter of compromise was quickly becoming one of inflexible law. Moreover, as the sensibilities of society became more refined, it became clear to the neutral observer that the height of the moral ground held by the landowners resembled a rather deep pit. Unlike fox-hunting, it was difficult to justify the killing of grouse on the grounds that you were ridding your land of predatory vermin. So, equally inevitably, the call for a return to unlimited access became irresistible.

In fact, it was the way that the fingers of history had kept a grip on this land that most summed up the journey. The whole affair was a bit of an archaeological dig. For some, if not much of the time, I must have been walking in the steps of my hunter-gatherer ancestors, following tracks that followed tracks that followed theirs. On this palimpsest had been overprinted a social form and shape laid down by the Romans and hardened by the Anglo-Saxons and Danes, which in due course threw up a chain of mediaeval castles, now ruined by cannon shot and north-east gales, and market towns with their cobbled squares and packhorse tracks. But overriding are the scars of those alchemists of the Industrial Revolution who, with their network of canals and railway lines, managed to turn base metals, ripped from the hillside, into the golden egg of Empire. Each age has left its mark. Some, like Hadrian's Wall, have been preserved and cherished, others left for nature to heal in its rank and random manner.

But there were times when I felt the real North was the sum of the people I met. The refrain was consistent: *They can change names, but not folk.* Although the shifting sands of boundary permutation make those of Morecambe Bay appear like bedrock, those 'folk' who by birth and occupation have never left the land of their fathers still seem to have a strong sense of where they belong. Even those who have left will firmly proclaim their allegiance to their native heath, and to this day sporting fathers rush their very expectant wives to their county of choice, while the off-comers, as with all the converted, patiently explain the merits of living where they do. Maybe the old characters are no longer there, the rat-catcher of Ted Hughes, or Ben Rose of North Lees who, similarly, earned his Sunday 'lunch' by taking bets he could kill, skin and dress a lamb during the time it took for the Hathersage church clock to strike twelve.

Even so, *Things are not what they were* has been a lamentation of every succeeding generation. The telling differences are still there. Between Lancashire and Yorkshire, Northumberland and Durham, the North and its neighbours. For most, the choice of favouring the football teams of Newcastle or Sunderland, or distinguishing the merits of Herdwicks or Cheviots is no choice at all and you have to be brought up well

north of Birmingham before you can truly understand the real difference between Rugby Union and
Rugby League. Evidence of schism can even be found
in a single word. 'Canny', north of the Border, means
'shrewd', with perhaps a hint of cunning. A few miles
south, it is the ultimate seal of approbation: to the
Geordie nation a 'canny lad' is a man to be trusted, a
man of honour and generosity.

But, overall, the journey was personal and,
inevitably, nostalgic. I revisited places first met long
ago. The cairn of Helvellyn, my earliest excursion
beyond the coastal flatlands. Crag Lough, Wasdale
and Stanage, where the climbing began, then caught
me by surprise. Inns like those at Langdon Beck and
Tan Hill, hearths of celebration and ports in storm.
Heads of rivers that flow through long-hewn and half
forgotten passages towards the parks of Ayresome,
St James and the late lamented Roker. And, in the
fullness of time, bits of the Bob Graham, Three Peaks,
and Marsden–Edale, old challenges, now once more
crossed, joined and left. Then the last stroll down a
stony track to an old bridge where a young child once
made a bit of a splash.

Those who can, do. Those who can't, think
wistfully.

The route
Tops of the North, Volumes I and II

In order to help route planning, this itinerary has been divided into a series of stages, each with an *approximate* mileage. The distance given does not take into account the terrain or, when there is a choice, the route chosen by the individual and should only be regarded as a rough guide. Most, but by no means all, of these stages can be broken into shorter days, either by staying in accommodation en route or using public transport. The information on offer is:

1   Points of DEPARTURE and ARRIVAL, with approximate mileage.
2   These to enclose **points** on the route, where either accommodation or public transport is available to offer a shorter day.
3   Other points situated on the route—summits, villages, pubs, etc—to indicate the general line of travel.
4   Each *COUNTY TOP,* old or new.
5   Identification of Long Distance Routes (LDRs) coincident with part or all of the stage, *Waymarked* or merely *Recorded.*

Stage One *(Vol I, Chapter 1)*
   THREE SHIRE HEAD—Cat and Fiddle—*SHINING TOR*—Pym Chair—Taxal Moor—**Whaley Bridge**—Chinley Churn—Hills Farm—Edale Cross—Upper Booth—EDALE (19 miles) LDRs: *Pennine Way, Macclesfield–Edale*

Stage Two *(Vol I, Chapter 1)*

EDALE—Ringing Roger—*KINDER SCOUT*—Mill Hill
—Snake Road—Bleaklow Head—CROWDEN (16 miles)
LDR: *Pennine Way*

Stage Three *(Vol I, Chapters 1–2)*

CROWDEN—*BLACK CHEW HEAD*—*BLACK HILL*—
Wassenden Head—**Marsden**—Tunnel End—Ram's Head
Inn—M62—Hollingworth Lake—LITTLEBOROUGH
(20 miles) LDRs: *Pennine Way, Station to Station Walk,
Rochdale Way*

Stage Four *(Vol I, Chapter 2)*

LITTLEBOROUGH—King William IV—Watergrove
Reservoir—Brown Wardle Hill—Hades Hill—A68—
Thievely Pike—Dyneley Farm—Towneley Hall—
BURNLEY (15 miles) LDRs: *Rossendale Way, Burnley Way*

Stage Five *(Vol I, Chapter 3)*

BURNLEY—Higham—Newchurch—Pendle Hill—
Downham—**Sawley**—Brown Hill—SLAIDBURN
(21 miles) LDRs: *Burnley Way, Pendle Way, Witches Way*

Stage Six *(Vol I, Chapter 4–5)*

SLAIDBURN—Higher Wood House—Salter Fell—High
Salter—**Wray**—HORNBY (16 miles) LDRs: *Witches Way,
North Bowland Traverse*

Stage Seven *(Vol I, Chapter 5)*

HORNBY—Loyn Bridge—Aughton—Nether Kellett—
M6—Lancaster Canal—**Carnforth**—Warton—Leighton
Hall— Yealand Conyers—Leighton Moss Nature Reserve
—Silverdale—Arnside Knott—ARNSIDE (19 miles)
LDRs: *None*

Stage Eight *(Vol I, Chapters 5–6)*

ARNSIDE—Morecambe Bay—Kents Bank—Humphrey
Head—Sand Gate—**Cark**—CARTMEL (15 miles)

LDRs: Cumbria Coastal Way, Cistercian Way

Stage Nine *(Vol I, Chapter 6)*

CARTMEL—Wall Nook—Bigland Tarn—Haverthwaite—Dicksons Arms—**Red Lion, Lowick**—Nibthwaite—Top o' Selside—Grizedale Forest—Brantwood—CONISTON (24 miles) LDR: *Furness Way*

Stage Ten *(Vol I, Chapter 7 and Interlude)*

CONISTON—*CONISTON OLD MAN*—Swirl How—Wrynose Pass—Crinkle Crags—*SCAFELL PIKE*—Rossett Ghyll—Mickleden—LANGDALE (19 miles) LDR: *Cumbria Way*

Stage Eleven *(Vol I, Chapter 8)*

LANGDALE—Stickle Tarn—Pavey Ark—High Raise—Steel Fell—Dunmail Raise—Grisedale Tarn—Dollywagon Pike—*HELVELLYN*—Watson Dod—Great Dod—THRELKELD (18 miles) LDRs: *None*

Stage Twelve *(Vol I, Chapter 8)*

THRELKELD—Skiddaw House—Peter House Farm—Orthwaite—Longlands—Branthwaite—Nether Row—CALDBECK (19 miles) LDR: *Cumbria Way*

Stage Thirteen *(Vol I, Envoi)*

CALDBECK—Sebergham—Rose Bridge—Bridge End—**Dalston**—Cummersdale—CARLISLE (15 miles) LDR: *Cumbria Way*

Stage Fourteen *(Vol II, Chapter 1)*

CARLISLE—Rickerby—Crosby-on-Eden—Newtown—WALTON (11 miles) LDR: *Hadrian's Wall Path*

Stage Fifteen *(Vol II, Chapter 1)*

WALTON—Birdoswald—**Greenhead**—Walltown Crags—Caw Gap—Winshields Crag—Steel Rigg—TWICE BREWED INN (16 miles) LDRs: *Hadrian's Wall Path, Pennine Way*

Stage Sixteen *(Vol II, Chapter 2)*

    TWICE BREWED INN—Crag Lough—Rapishaw Gap—Wark Forest—Horneystead Farm—Shitlington—BELLINGHAM (18 miles) LDRs: ***Hadrian's Wall Path, Pennine Way***

Stage Seventeen *(Vol II, Chapter 2)*

    BELLINGHAM—Hareshaw House—Whitley Pike—Redesdale Forest—Blakehopeburnhaugh—BYRNESS (16 miles) LDR: ***Pennine Way***

Stage Eighteen *(Vol II, Chapter 2)*

    BYRNESS—Chew Green—Lamb Hill—Mozie Law—Windy Gyle—USWAYFORD (15 miles) LDR: ***Pennine Way***

Stage Nineteen *(Vol II, Chapter 2)*

    USWAYFORD—Windy Gyle—Kings Seat—*THE CHEVIOT*—Scald Hill—Broadstruther—Watch Hill—WOOLER (18 miles) LDRs: ***Pennine Way, St Cuthbert's Way,*** *Reivers Way*

Stage Twenty *(Vol II, Chapter 2)*

    WOOLER—Weetwood Bridge—East Horton—St Cuthbert's Cave—Swinhoe Farm—**Belford**—Waren Mill—BAMBURGH (18 miles) LDRs: *St Cuthbert's Way, St Oswald's Way, Reivers Way*

Stage Twenty One *(Vol II, Chapter 3)*

    BAMBURGH—**Seahouses**—Beadnell—Low Newton—CRASTER (14 miles) LDRs: *St Oswald's Way, Reivers Way*

Stage Twenty Two *(Vol II, Chapter 3)*

    CRASTER—Boulmer—**Alnmouth**—WARKWORTH (13 miles) LDR: *St Oswald's Way*

Stage Twenty Three *(Vol II, Chapter 3)*

    WARKWORTH—**Felton**—**Weldon Bridge**—Pauperhaugh—ROTHBURY (18 miles) LDR: *St Oswald's Way*

Stage Twenty Four *(Vol II, Chapter 3)*

ROTHBURY—Lordenshaws—Fallowlees—Harwood—Catcherside—Knowesgate—KIRKWHELPINGTON (15 miles) LDR: *St Oswald's Way*

Stage Twenty Five *(Vol II, Chapter 3)*

KIRKWHELPINGTON—Great Bavington—Little Bavington—Hallington—Great Whittington—Errington Arms—Heavenfield—WALL (19 miles) LDRs: *St Oswald's Way, Hadrian's Wall Path*

Stage Twenty Six *(Vol II, Chapters 3–4)*

WALL—Acomb—**Hexham**—Dipton Mill Inn—Greenridge—Gaterley Hill—**Allendale Town**—Park Farm— Knockburn Farm—Dirt Pot—ALLENHEADS (25 miles) LDR: *Isaac's Tea Trail*

Stage Twenty Seven *(Vol II, Chapter 4)*

ALLENHEADS—Killhope Law—Killhope Cross—Nag's Head—Dead Stones—*BURNHOPE SEAT*—B6277—Cow Green Reservoir—LANGDON BECK (20 miles) LDRs: *None*

Stage Twenty Eight *(Vol II, Chapter 4)*

LANGDON BECK—Cauldron Snout—Birkdale Farm—Moss Shop—Maize Beck—*MICKLE FELL*—Hanging Seal—B6276—Dow Crag—Pind Hill—Balderhead Reservoir—BALDERSDALE (23 miles) LDRs: *None*

Stage Twenty Nine *(Vol II, Chapter 4)*

BALDERSDALE—Race Yat—A66—God's Bridge—TAN HILL INN (10 miles) LDR: *Pennine Way*

NB It is possible to compress the last two stages into one by following the County Boundary over Round Hill, Great Dodd and Beldoo Hill before crossing the A66 and continuing over Bowes Moor to the Tan Hill Inn (25 miles).

Stage Thirty *(Vol II, Chapter 5)*
TAN HILL INN—**Kirkby Stephen**—Smardale Bridge—
Ravenstonedale—Green Bell—Randygill Top—The
Calf—SEDBERGH (28 miles) LDR: *Coast to Coast*

Stage Thirty One *(Vol II, Chapter 5)*
SEDBERGH—**Dent**—*GRAGARETH*—*WHERNSIDE*
—Ingleborough—Hill Inn—HORTON-IN-RIBBLES-
DALE (21 miles) LDRs: *Dales Way, Yorkshire Dales
Centurion Walk*

Stage Thirty Two *(Vol II, Chapter 5)*
HORTON-IN-RIBBLESDALE—Pen-y-ghent—Foxup
—**Arncliffe**—KETTLEWELL (15 miles) LDR: *Yorkshire
Dales Centurion Walk*

Stage Thirty Three *(Vol II, Chapter 6)*
KETTLEWELL—**Grassington**—Bolton Abbey—
Addingham—ILKLEY (23 miles) LDR: *Dales Way*

Stage Thirty Four *(Vol II, Chapter 6)*
ILKLEY—White Wells—Lanshaw Lad—Weecher Reser-
voir—Glovershaw—Shipley Glen—**Saltaire**—Beckfoot
—Goitstock Wood—A629—**Oxenhope**—Leeshaw
Reservoir—Stair—New Bridge—**Pecket Well**—Crow
Hill—MYTHOLMROYD (27 miles) LDRs: *Bradford
Millennium Way, Calderdale Way, Yorkshire Water Way*

Stage Thirty Five *(Vol II, Chapter 6)*
MYTHOLMROYD—Stake Lane—Slate Delfs Hill—
Great Manshead Hill—A58—Baitings Reservoir—Booth
Wood Reservoir—M62—Deanhead Reservoir—Cupwith
Reservoir—MARSDEN (14 miles) LDRs: *Calderdale Way,
Kirklees Way, Yorkshire Water Way*

Stage Thirty Six *(Vol II, Chapter 6)*
MARSDEN—Butterley Reservoir—Wessenden Head—
Digley Reservoir—**Holme**—Ramsden Reservoir—Winscar

Reservoir—Dunford Bridge—FLOUCH INN (16 miles)
LDRs: *Pennine Way, Kirklees Way,* Yorkshire Water Way

Stage Thirty Seven *(Vol II, Chapter 7)*

FLOUCH INN—Howden Edge—*MARGERY HILL*—
Dovestones Tor—Cutthroat Bridge—Mosacar Lodge—
Stanage Edge—Burbage Edge—**Fox House Inn**—Froggatt
Edge—Froggatt Bridge—EYAM (24 miles) LDRs: *None*

Stage Thirty Eight *(Vol II, Chapter 7)*

EYAM—**Foolow**—Wardlow Mires—Cressbrook
Dale—**Millers Dale**—Chee Dale—Blackwell—A6—
Chelmorton—Deepdale—Cowdale—Buxton Country
Park—Axe Edge Moor—*CHEEKS HILL*—THREE
SHIRE HEAD (19 miles) LDRs: *Monsal Trail, Dane
Valley Way*

Various 'Way' publications

The following (given current state of publication) may be of use when planning the various stages of the route. Similar details for Stages One–Thirteen appear in Volume I.

Stage Fourteen–Stage Thirty Eight

Pennine Way, Edward de la Billiere and Keith Carter, Trailblazer Publications

Hadrian's Wall Path, Anthony Burton, Aurum Press

St Cuthbert's Way, Roger Smith and Ron Shaw, Kelso Graphics

The Reivers Way, James Roberts, Cicerone Press

St Oswald's Way, Malcolm Paminter, Alnwick District Council

Isaac's Tea Trail, Roger Morris, City Print Services

A Coast to Coast Walk, Alfred Wainwright, Westmorland Gazette

The Yorkshire Dales Centurion Way, Jonathan Ginesi, John Siddall (Printers) Ltd

The Dales Way, Terry Marsh, Cicerone Press

Bradford's Millennium Way, ed Jim Thornber, Birch Printers (Bradford) Ltd

Trans-Pennine Way, Paul Hannon, Hillside Publications

Calderdale Way, Paul Hannon, Hillside Publications

The Kirklees Way, C Dexter Ellis, 4 Prospect Place, Holmfirth HD7 1RH

The Yorkshire Water Way, Mark Reid, Innway Publications

Monsal Trail, Peak District National Park, Baslow Road, Bakewell DE45 1AE

Dane Valley Way, R M Lloyd, Congleton Tourist Information Service, Congleton

Selected bibliography

Bibby, A: *South Pennines and the Brontë Moors* (Frances Lincoln, 2005)

Bibby, A: *The Backbone of England* (Frances Lincoln, 2008)

Bonney, S: *Fifty Favourite Northumbrian Pubs* ('The Northumbrian' magazine, 2008)

Dillon, P: *Walking in The North Pennines* (Cicerone Press, 1991)

Durham, K: *The Border Reivers* (Osprey Publishing, 1995)

Edgar, J (ed): *An Accessible Wilderness* (Derbyshire County Council/Peak District National Park Authority, 2003)

Hewitt, P: *Bronte Country* (Sutton Publishing, 2004)

Gould, D: *A Short History of Chelmorton* (D Gould, 2007)

Hayes, G: *Odd Corners around the Howgills* (Hayloft Publishing, 2004)

Hugill, R: *Borderland Castles and Peles* (Sandhill Press, 1996)

Raistrick, A: *Mines and Miners of Swaledale* (Dalesman Publishing, 1955)

Rudd, MDC: *The Discovery of Teesdale* (Phillimore & Co, 2007)

Smith, K: *Emperor of Industry* (Tynebridge Publishing, 2005)

Turnbull, L: *The History of Leadmining in the North East of England* (Ergo Press, 2006)

For a complete list of Millrace books
on climbing, hill walking, and
travel in the past, visit

www.millracebooks.co.uk